Navigating
Boundaries

Recent Titles in the
Praeger Series in Political Communication
Robert E. Denton, Jr., General Editor

Navigating Boundaries

The Rhetoric of
Women Governors

Edited by
Brenda DeVore Marshall
and Molly A. Mayhead

Praeger Series in Political Communication

PRAEGER　　　　　　　　　　Westport, Connecticut
London

Library of Congress Cataloging-in-Publication Data

Navigating boundaries : the rhetoric of women governors / edited by Brenda DeVore
Marshall and Molly A. Mayhead.
    p.   cm.—(Praeger series in political communication, ISSN 1062–5623)
    Includes bibliographical references and index.
    ISBN 0–275–96778–6 (alk. paper)—ISBN 0–275–96779–4 (pbk. : alk. paper)
    1. Political oratory—United States. 2. Women governors—United States. I.
Marshall, Brenda DeVore, 1951– II. Mayhead, Molly A., 1961– III. Series.
PN4193.P6 N38 2000
808.5′1′089351—dc21   99–059513

British Library Cataloguing in Publication Data is available.

Library of Congress Catalog Card Number: 99–059513
ISBN: 0–275–96778–6
    0–275–96779–4 (pbk.)
ISSN: 1062–5623

First published in 2000

Praeger Publishers, 88 Post Road West, Westport, CT 06881
An imprint of Greenwood Publishing Group, Inc.
www.praeger.com

Printed in the United States of America

The paper used in this book complies with the
Permanent Paper Standard issued by the National
Information Standards Organization (Z39.48–1984).

10 9 8 7 6 5 4 3 2 1

Contents

Series Foreword

Those of us from the discipline of communication studies have long believed that communication is prior to all other fields of inquiry. In several other forums I have argued that the essence of politics is "talk" or human interaction.[1] Such interaction may be formal or informal, verbal or nonverbal, public or private, but it is always persuasive, forcing us consciously or subconsciously to interpret, to evaluate, and to act. Communication is the vehicle for human action.

From this perspective, it is not surprising that Aristotle recognized the natural kinship of politics and communication in his writings *Politics* and *Rhetoric*. In the former, he established that humans are "political beings, [who] alone of the animals [are] furnished with the faculty of language."[2] In the latter, he began his systematic analysis of discourse by proclaiming that "rhetorical study, in its strict sense, is concerned with the modes of persuasion."[3] Thus, it was recognized over twenty-three hundred years ago that politics and communication go hand in hand because they are essential parts of human nature.

In 1981, Dan Nimmo and Keith Sanders proclaimed that political communication was an emerging field.[4] Although its origin, as noted, dates back centuries, a "self-consciously cross-disciplinary" focus began in the late 1950s. Thousands of books and articles later, colleges and universities offer a variety of graduate and undergraduate coursework in the area in such diverse departments as communication, mass communication, journalism, political science, and sociology.[5] In Nimmo and Sander's early assessment, the "key areas of inquiry" included rhetorical analysis, propaganda analysis, attitude change studies, voting studies, government and the news media, functional and systems analyses, technological changes, media technologies, campaign techniques, and research techniques.[6] In a survey of the state of the field in 1983, the same authors and Lynda Kaid found additional, more specific areas of concerns such as the presidency polls, public opinion, debates, and advertising.[7] Since the first study, they have also noted a shift away from the rather strict behavioral approach.

A decade later, Dan Nimmo and David Swanson argued that "political communication has development some identity as a more or less distinct domain of scholarly work."[8] The scope and concerns of the area have further expanded to include critical theories and cultural studies. Although there is no precise definition, method, or disciplinary home of the area of inquiry, its primary domain comprises the role, processes, and effects of communication within the context of politics broadly defined.

In 1985, the editors of *Political Communication Yearbook: 1984* noted that "more things are happening in the study, teaching, and practice of political communication than can be captured within the space limitations of the relatively few publications available."[9] In addition, they argued that the backgrounds of "those involved in the field [are] so varied and pluralist in outlook and approach, . . . it [is] a mistake to adhere slavishly to any set format in shaping the content."[10] More recently, Swanson and Nimmo have called for "ways of overcoming the unhappy consequences of fragmentation within a framwork that respects, encourages, and benefits from diverse scholarly commitments, agendas, and approaches."[11]

In agreement with these assessments of the area and with gentle encouragement, in 1988 Praeger established the series entitled "Praeger Series in Political Communication." The series is open to all qualitative and quantitive methodologies as well as contemporary and historical studies. The key to characterizing the studies in the series is the focus on communication variables or activities within a political context or dimension. As of this writing, over seventy volumes have been published and numerous impressive works are forthcoming. Scholars from the disciplines of communication, history, journalism, political science, and sociology have participated in the series.

I am, without shame or modesty, a fan of the series. The joy of serving as its editor is in participating in the dialogue of the field of political communication and in reading the contributors' works. I invite you to join me.

Robert E. Denton, Jr.

NOTES

1. See Robert E. Denton, Jr., *The Symbolic Dimensions of the American Presidency* (Prospect Heights, IL: Waveland Press, 1982); Robert E. Denton, Jr.,

and Gary Woodward, *Political Communication in America* (New York: Praeger, 1985; 2d ed., 1990); Robert E. Denton, Jr., and Dan Hahn. *Presidential Communication* (New York: Praeger, 1986); and Robert E. Denton Jr., *The Primetime Presidency of Ronald Regan* (New York: Praeger, 1988).

2. Aristotle, *The Politics of Aristotle*, trans. Ernest Barker (New York: Oxford University Press, 1970), p. 5

3. Aristotle, *Rhetoric*, trans. W. Rhys Roberts (New York: The Modern Library, 1954), p. 22.

4. Dan Nimmo and Keith Sanders, "Introduction: The Emergence of Political Communication as a Field," in *Handbook of Political Communication*, eds Dan Nimmo and Keith Sanders (Beverly Hills, CA: Sage, 1981), pp. 11–36.

5. Ibid., p. 15.

6. Ibid., pp. 17–27.

7. Keith Sanders, Lynda Kaid, and Dan Nimmo, eds. *Political Communication Yearbook*: 1984 (Carbondale, IL: Southern Illinois Univeristy: 1985), pp. 283–308.

8. Dan Nimmo and David Swanson, "The Field of Political Communication: Beyond the Voter Persuasion Paradigm," in *New Directions in Political Communication*, eds. David Swanson and Dan Nimmo (Beverly Hills, CA: Sage, 1990), p. 8.

9. Sanders, Kaid, and Nimmo, *Political Communication Yearbook*: *1984*, p. xiv.

10. Ibid.

11. Nimmo and Swanson, "The Field of Political Communication," p. 11.

Acknowledgments

We wish to express our gratitude and debt to the female pioneers, both historical and contemporary, who courageously found and continue to find ways to make their voices heard in the political arena. We also thank our colleagues, both female and male, whose previous works have made the study of women's discourse a more integral part of our discipline. And, we deeply appreciate the contributions made to this project by Kristina Horn Sheeler, Jennifer Burek Pierce, Alma Hall, and Shannon Skarphol Kaml.

Alma Hall wishes to thank Governor Martha Layne Collins, the subject of this research, who has afforded her new insight into the effective leadership of women. Humble by nature, Governor Collins continues to work tirelessly "for Kentucky" and obviously prefers that work to talking about her successes. Nevertheless, she opened her memory and her files to Alma out of a dedication to the young women who will follow her. Second, Alma thanks her colleagues in the Department of Communication Arts at Georgetown College who have offered her encouragement on this project: Ed Smith, Jayne Violette, Regina Francies, George McGee, and Margaret Greynolds. Finally, she thanks her students and her daughters, Hope and J. J., who inspire her to keep learning.

Shannon Skarphol Kaml dedicates her work to Grandpa Winton who would have liked to read even more about Populism.

Jennifer Burek Pierce wishes to thank Professor Michael Salvador of Washington State University, whose graduate seminar in rhetorical criticism resulted in an early draft of "Portrait of a 'Governor Lady,'" and Professor J. Michael Hogan of Pennsylvania State University, who also provided feedback on the essay, for their support and guidance of this project.

Kristina Horn Sheeler wishes to thank Brenda DeVore Marshall and Molly Mayhead for their tireless efforts in conceptualizing, organizing, and editing this project and also for their suggestions, encouragement, and reading of earlier drafts. Special thanks also go to Robert Ivie and John Lucaites for reading earlier versions of her essays and offering valuable feedback.

Molly Mayhead wishes to thank her parents, Janeen and Derek Mayhead, for their encouragement of and excitement about her work throughout her many years of education. She also wishes to thank her husband, Ed Dover, for his helpful suggestions throughout the writing process. Finally, she wishes to thank profusely her co-editor, Brenda DeVore Marshall, for being such an excellent colleague and friend.

Brenda DeVore Marshall wishes to thank her mother, Alberta Bowyer DeVore, for a lifetime of encouragement; her father, Keith DeVore, who throughout his life acknowledged the valuable role that women play in our world; and her aunt, Alene DeVore, for providing a role model for women in the public sphere. She also wishes to thank her colleague Barbara Seidman for her friendship, support, and insightful suggestions regarding portions of this project. And, she thanks Molly Mayhead for a truly collaborative experience and for her friendship. Finally, she wishes to thank her husband, Tyrone Marshall, for his love, friendship, and encouragement in all that she does.

The material in Kristina Horn Sheeler's chapters was originally developed as sections of her dissertation, "Women's Public Discourse and the Gendering of Leadership Culture: Ann Richards and Christine Todd Whitman Negotiate the Governorship," to be completed at Indiana University in 2000. Also, we are grateful to Governor Ann Richards for the use of portions of her speeches.

Introduction

> The rhetorical history of women tells the story of the nine-
> teenth-century struggle to obtain the right to speak and to function as
> moral agents. The struggle demonstrates that public speaking and fem-
> ininity were perceived as mutually exclusive. Because gender roles
> persist, contemporary women who seek leadership positions face bar-
> riers that make it particularly difficult for them to succeed
> —Campbell and Jerry 123

American women have come a long way in the last one hundred years. We
occupy positions as doctors, lawyers, astronauts, college professors, CEOs,
and politicians. However, on the brink of the twenty-first century, women
still encounter many of the obstacles faced by their predecessors. "Women
remain almost entirely excluded from power in political, economic, and
cultural institutions of importance in the United States, despite the small
gains of 'the year of the woman' [1992]" (Tronto 2). Nowhere are these barriers to public life greater than in the contemporary political arena. And no
political context in the United States is more fraught with challenges than
that faced by female governors.

While women are being elected to state and national legislatures at a
slightly increasing rate in recent decades, the number of women who consider entering a gubernatorial race, and ultimately those who succeed, is
much smaller. As Gertrude Mongella notes in the foreword to Brill's *A Rising Public Voice*, "in spite of the general increase in political participation
by women over the past twenty years, the overall numbers of women at the

highest levels of government remain unacceptably low" (xi). Although Brill's work focuses on women's participation in the national and international political hierarchy, Mongella's words ring true for state government as well. In the 224 years since the founding of the country, only sixteen women have served as governors. This book is a testament to and an analysis of the rhetoric of several of those women who have held their state's highest office and thus transformed the political landscape.

This project began in a most unlikely place—a forensics tabulation room. While computing tournament results, we discussed our common interest in the discourse of Ann Richards, then Governor of Texas, and Barbara Roberts, Governor of Oregon. We continued our dialogue by interrogating Roberts' rhetorical responses to her state's budget crisis. Intrigued by our early findings, we proposed a seminar series focusing on the rhetoric of women governors for the 1998 National Communication Association Convention and subsequently issued a call for papers. Our experience at the seminar and continued review of literature in the discipline convinced us that the rhetoric of gubernatorial women had been given scant attention to date and merited further inquiry.

Political discourse has, of course, held the attention of scholars for decades; in fact, the history of rhetoric in both Western and Eastern traditions is principally a history of political discourse. Our journals and bookshelves are replete with works analyzing the rhetorical successes and failures of a variety of historical and contemporary candidates and officeholders. Some books, like Kathleen Hall Jamieson's *Eloquence in an Electronic Age* and *Packaging the Presidency,* represent the finest in the field's examination of the fusion of campaigns and rhetoric. Yet, this scholarly tradition has been built primarily on the study of male politicians. Thus, we "have been given, at best, an impoverished view of women's role in advocating social, moral, cultural, economic and political change" (Kennedy and O'Shields xvii). While historical studies of women public speakers have appeared sporadically throughout this century, only recently have scholars begun seriously and systematically to consider the discourse of their female contemporaries who seek or hold office or who attempt to alter the political and social climate either locally or nationally. While more extensive surveys of the history of women's political discourse may be found in other works, the following selective overview of the literature illustrates this phenomenon.

Doris Yoakam's 1935 doctoral dissertation marked the beginning of formal academic interest in the efforts of American women to gain access to the public platform. "Her work presented for the first time the stirring details of the struggle by women in the ante-bellum period for acceptance as public speakers in the United States" (O'Connor viii). Yoakam's work illustrated that "these pioneer women risked their reputations by speaking out on the controversial issues of the day" (O'Connor viii).

Not long after, W. Norwood Brigance declared in his now classic two-volume work *A History and Criticism of American Public Address* published in 1943 that history "is made with words." Though he made clear that he would be "concerned with men who have used words to direct the course of American history," Brigance also included an essay devoted to the history of women's public speaking, claiming that "the emergence of women on the American platform was so distinctive a phase of history that it seemed best to give it fitting emphasis in a separate chapter" (I, vii–viii). Drawn from her doctoral dissertation, Doris Yoakam's essay, "Woman's Introduction to the American Platform," traced the emergence of women's voices in the public sphere from the 1830s through the end of the Civil War. Yoakam contended that "the first period of women's oratory in America assumes a significance that has been flagrantly neglected" (187). She argued that "in claiming the public platform for their use, the pioneer women orators set the precedent for and helped to establish the propriety of women as participants in and not merely spectators of public life" (187). Yet, despite the prominent forum Brigance had provided for such work, from the 1940s until the 1980s articles and books about women's political rhetoric appeared only sporadically.

In their 1954 publication *American Speeches*, Parrish and Hochmuth purported to "acquaint beginning students of public speaking with some of the great speeches of America's best speakers" and to provide "students of American oratory . . . some of the speeches that have been most influential in shaping our ideals, our culture, and our history" (v). However, among the twenty-eight speeches included in the book, there was not a single speech by a woman. A year later in the third volume of *A History and Criticism of American Public Address*, Marie Hochmuth included one essay about an early woman orator in the eleven chapters devoted to individual speakers. Doris Yoakam Twichell's examination of Susan B. Anthony's rhetoric marked the beginning of investigation into the public discourse of individual women in a manner consistent with the rhetorical criticism of their male counterparts. As Yoakam Twichell noted, Susan B. Anthony "was a classic example of the importance of the individual in public speaking" (130).

Lillian O'Connor published her groundbreaking work *Pioneer Women Orators* in the early 1950s as well. Noting that her subjects were interested in causes such as slavery, temperance, and education, O'Connor analyzed the texts of twenty-seven women speakers (vii, 41) "to discover whether or not women of the early reform platform utilized *ethos, pathos,* and *logos* in the texts of their addresses." Furthermore, she asked, "if they did, whether or not there was any characteristic use of such rhetorical proof by the majority of the speakers" (O'Connor 230). O'Connor concluded that these speakers did indeed offer "rhetorical proof in the three acceptable modes" and that "the women must have had some acquaintance, either through study on their own part or because of the constant practice of public speaking around them, with the rhetorical standards and textbooks of the day" (225).

Not all scholars, however, were convinced of the sophistication that O'Connor claimed for women orators. Like Brigance, Robert Oliver included a discussion of women speakers in his 1965 work, *History of Public Speaking in America*, and like Yoakam and O'Connor, Oliver concentrated his discussion on the early pioneers. But, he asserted that with the few exceptions described in his essay, "the contribution of women, at least in the nineteenth century, to the public speaking platform, has largely been in numbers of passionate advocates and agitators, rather than in outstanding individual achievement" (447).

In the midst of the resurgence of women's political and social activism, the 1970s witnessed the appearance of additional rhetorical studies of historical and contemporary movements relevant to the lives of women. These included Martha Solomon's "The 'Positive Woman's' Journey: A Mythic Analysis of the Rhetoric of STOP ERA" and Sonja Foss's "Equal Rights Amendment Controversy: Two Worlds in Conflict." DeWitte Holland included Coleman's analysis, "Suffrage and Prohibition: Integrated Issues," in his book, *America in Controversy: History of American Public Address*. In Waldo Braden's 1979 collection of essays titled *Oratory in the New South*, Annette Shelby investigated the reform speaking of native southern women from 1870 to 1920. She argued that "by the early 1870s, [southern women reformers] were speaking increasingly before southern audiences and exerting influence there far beyond that commonly imagined" (205). These works reflected an emerging trend in rhetorical criticism—the interrogation of both historical and contemporary political discourse.

In *Feminist Rhetorical Theories*, Karen Foss, Sonja Foss, and Cindy Griffin maintain that Karlyn Kohrs Campbell's "The Rhetoric of Women's Liberation" announced the emergence of feminist perspectives in the study of rhetoric and public address. Campbell argued that "the rhetoric of women's liberation is a distinctive genre because it evinces unique rhetorical qualities that are a fusion of substantive and stylistic features" (75). Foss, Foss, and Griffin have noted that "Campbell's article constituted the first effort to reconceptualize theoretical constructs from a feminist perspective, a focus of feminist scholarship that would not appear again for many years" (15).

Karlyn Kohrs Campbell's subsequent work in the 1980s established her leadership in the analysis of women's political rhetoric. These included articles such as "Stanton's 'The Solitude of Self': A Rationale for Feminism," "Style and Content in the Rhetoric of Early Afro-American Feminists," and "Woman and Speaker: A Conflict in Roles," co-authored with E. Claire Jerry. Her two-volume work, *Man Cannot Speak for Her,* provided a historical look at women speakers throughout the nineteenth and early twentieth centuries. Arguing that it is "clear that the rhetoric of women must be studied if we are to understand human symbolization in all its variety" (9), Campbell has provided scholars with an in-depth survey of major speakers in the early part of the woman's rights movement. In this work, Campbell also took the daring step of identifying the characteristics of a "feminine style" in the discourse of these activists. In embracing a model of discourse that incorporated women's experiences and perspectives, she provided grounding for much of the study of women's political rhetoric in the 1990s.

As women's participation in the public arena increased in the 1980s, more scholars turned their attention to the political discourse of these modern pioneers. This work included Wayne N. Thompson's investigation of Barbara Jordan's 1976 keynote address to the Democratic National Convention and Patricia Witherspoon's examination of Jordon's statement before the House Judiciary Committee on the impeachment of Richard Nixon. In 1988, Victoria O'Donnell contributed a fantasy-theme analysis of Geraldine Ferraro's 1984 vice-presidential acceptance speech to the scholarly conversation on women's oratory. Patricia Sullivan also focused on Ferraro's rhetoric in her 1989 article, "The 1984 Vice-Presidential Debate: A Case Study of Female and Male Framing in Political Campaigns."

In their 1987 article, "Women in Communication Studies: A Typology for Revision," Carole Spitzack and Kathryn Carter followed Campbell's lead in arguing for a paradigm shift that allows women's voices to be included in the canon *and* that redefines the dominant worldview that leads to canon creation in the first place. Similarly, Catherine Dobris noted in 1989 that "increased visibility of women in the public sphere does not necessarily mean that women's communication experiences, whether private or public, are valued within the dominant culture" since "our theories have assumed a relatively stable picture of humanity which does not include women" (137–138). Answering her own call and reflecting Campbell's 1973 dictum, Dobris developed a rhetorical theory that accounts for gender—a theory that assumed that male models are not the only models (156).

The year 1983 marked the appearance of the first anthology of women's speeches in this country, Kennedy and O'Shields's *We Shall Be Heard: Women Speakers in America, 1928–Present.* Two years later, Judith Anderson produced another collection, *Outspoken Women: Speeches by American Women Reformers, 1635–1936*. In 1987, Bernard Duffy and Halford Ryan included studies of four women speakers in their *American Orators before 1900: Critical Studies and Sources*. They replicated this model with the inclusion of analyses of five women rhetors in *American Orators of the Twentieth Century*.

Continuing the trend begun in the 1980s, several noteworthy articles and books in the past decade have delved into the topic of contemporary women's political rhetoric. In his 1995 dissertation, for instance, David Sullivan examined the campaigns of three women gubernatorial candidates in the 1990 election—Dianne Feinstein in California, Evelyn Murphy in Massachusetts, and Ann Richards in Texas—and identified "the processes by which the formal elements of campaign discourse mediate the different voice women candidates bring to electoral politics" (4). Continuing his research of Dianne Feinstein's rhetoric, Sullivan analyzed her public image in three political campaigns from 1990 to 1994 in his "Images of a Breakthrough Candidate." He posited that women candidates such as Feinstein are aided by the shift from print to electronic sources, for they are better able to redefine and present their image in the electronic media. Sullivan's article demonstrates the now predominant pratice of focusing on one candidate using case study analysis.

Drawing on the increasing intersection between public discourse and the media, Judith Trent and Robert Friedenberg, in *Political Campaign Communication*, argued that "one of the most interesting aspects of televised political advertising during the 1980s and early 1990s was the use of attack spots by female candidates" (135). These authors noted the double bind women face in negotiating the boundaries between traditional gender expectations and contemporary political realities. In addition, Trevor Parry-Giles and Shawn Parry-Giles studied gendered politics and presidential image construction in five presidential campaign films with "symbolically powerful constructions of masculinity expressed in a 'feminine' style" (338). They argued in "Gendered Politics and Presidential Image Construction: A Reassessment of the 'Feminine Style' " that "presidential image is constructed by the association of characteristics necessary for successful presidential leadership" and that "these films offer a portrayal of women that marginalizes their status in the political process" (337). Ultimately, they concluded that the presence of feminine style masks the presence of hegemonic construction of images "that serves to preserve politics as a patriarchal system" (337).

Illustrating the continuing interest in contemporary women's speeches, another anthology, Victoria DeFrancisco and Marvin Jensen's *Women's*

Voices in Our Time, appeared in 1994. Other works of interest include Janis King's 1990 study of the justificatory rhetoric of Wilma Mankiller, the first woman chief of the Cherokee nation. And, Patricia Sullivan extended past research with an investigation of Patricia Schroeder's rhetoric.

Reflecting on Campbell's work, Dow and Boor Tonn asserted that there is a feminine style in women's political discourse and that it "can function to offer alternative modes of political reasoning" (288). These authors suggested that Ann Richards' rhetoric enunciates a unique political philosophy that privileges care, nurturance, and relationships as the informing principles of governmental policy. Blankenship and Robson extended the interrogation of "feminine style" by looking at the discourse of congresswomen in campaign and governance contexts. In their article, "A 'Feminine Style' in Women's Political Discourse," they identified five characteristics of a feminine rhetorical style and mapped its growing prominence in the communication strategies of male and female candidates alike. Similarly, in *From the Margins to the Center: Contemporary Women and Political Communication*, Patricia Sullivan teamed with Lynn Turner to "discover how women are *redefining* the public leadership realm through their communication—both in their expressions of different experiences and in their choices of communication styles and strategies" (xviii).

In yet another two-volume collection, Karlyn Kohrs Campbell once again contributed to our historical understanding of women orators with her *Women Public Speakers in the United States, 1800–1925: A Bio-Critical Sourcebook* and *Women Public Speakers in the United States, 1925–1993: A Bio-Critical Sourcebook*. As noted in the second volume, Campbell focused on "the varied voices that emerged out of efforts to articulate women's condition and to seek change, or even impede it" (xvii). This collection of essays examined sixty-nine speakers from fields as diverse as politics, law, and literature. In his *African-American Orators: A Bio-Critical Sourcebook*, Richard Leeman included studies of fifteen African-American female rhetors. Following Leeman, Philip Foner and Robert Branham included the speeches of twenty-three women in *Lift Every Voice: African American Oratory, 1787–1900*. And, Shirley Wilson Logan expanded the study of the rhetoric of African-American women with her two books *With Pen and Voice: A Critical Anthology of Nineteenth-Century African-American Women* and *"We Are Coming": The Persuasive Discourse of Nineteenth-Century Black Women*.

This representative survey of studies of women's political rhetoric illustrates the steadily increasing interest in scholarship on the topic. However, there is little work treating the discourse of women governors and no in-depth collection of articles or essays examining the rhetoric of several women, over time, who have held the same office. This work attempts to bridge those gaps.

We have focused on five governors–Nellie Tayloe Ross, Martha Layne Collins, Ann Richards, Barbara Roberts, and Christine Todd Whitman–because collectively they represent the ever-changing and diverse face of the governorship. Other than gender, these governors have little in common. They come from diverse social and economic backgrounds and thus bring multiple personal views to the office. These varied perspectives also originate from the differences in time period, political affiliation, geographic location, and ideology that these women reflect.

The first chapter of this book discusses the changing face of the office of governor. From colonial times to the present, the position has evolved from that of a mere figurehead to a position of power and importance in both state and federal politics. A brief biographical sketch of each of the women who have held the governorship illustrates these changes as well as the common obstacles faced by women in different time periods.

In chapter 2, Kristina Horn Sheeler details metaphors used by the media to describe women governors throughout history. These images include pioneer, puppet, beauty queen, and unruly woman. She concludes that the metaphors are primarily negative and thus create yet another forum for marginalizing women and their ideas.

The autobiographical political advocacy of Nellie Tayloe Ross, the first woman elected to serve as governor, focuses the discussion in chapter 3. As early as the mid-1920s, Ross illustrated through her personal life, her public work, and her writings the link between women's private lives and the public sphere. Jennifer Burek Pierce examines the tensions between the perceived liberalism of a woman entering the political arena and her private convictions concerning women's domestic role.

Alma Hall analyzes the rhetoric of Martha Layne Collins in chapter 4. She posits a relationship between a leader's effectiveness and her ability to frame issues rhetorically to create identification with the electorate. Hall argues that during her term as governor, Collins created a shared vision of educational and economic reform for Kentucky that led to major positive changes for the state and its citizens.

According to Shannon Skarphol Kaml in chapter 5, Ann Richards' discourse blends both feminine style and populist rhetorical strategies. Richards employed the populist strategies of blame placing and the use of humor, irony, and sarcasm alongside the feminist characteristics of consensus building and caring. Kaml argues that this fusion enabled Richards to succeed in a state known for its masculine leadership models.

In chapter 6, we examine Barbara Roberts' political rhetoric in response to Oregon's budget crisis and suggest that previous studies do not go far enough in analyzing how women politicians negotiate entrenched political boundaries. Roberts' experience dramatizes the need for women leaders both to re-vision those existing boundaries and their accompanying discourse and to re-frame the rhetorical paradigms from which they operate. This re-framing allows the woman politician to morph the lines between hegemonic tradition and new horizons, ultimately creating novel strategies for transcending existing ideological constructs.

Focusing on Christine Todd Whitman's two inaugurals and selected radio addresses in the last chapter, Sheeler reveals the ideological underpinnings of Whitman's discourse. After discussing the gendered implications of political leadership, she considers the ways in which Whitman both reinforces existing ideologies and creates new political belief systems that are more amenable to both women and men. Sheeler concludes that Whitman "produces a hegemonic articulation that gives the impression of moving forward productively while offering no structural change."

We believe this book, with its analysis of the rhetoric of women governors, provides a needed examination of how these individuals used public discourse to attain or maintain their state's highest office. Because so few women have held the office of governor and since there are even fewer studies about the discourse of women governors, we trust that this book will generate new issues for discussion and evaluation of women's political rhetoric. In so doing, we hope to contribute to a broader understanding of the ways in which women navigate the often treacherous boundaries of contemporary politics.

Chapter One

The Changing Face of the Governorship

Brenda DeVore Marshall
and Molly A. Mayhead

In his chapter, which details the changing perspectives on the American governor, J. Oliver Williams posits that "the governor is the prime mover of significant politics and administration on the state level and much of inter-governmental politics can be interpreted through the gubernatorial role" (2). It is impossible to find a person in this country who has not been affected by the policies of state government or governors. Because of the impact of the state's highest office and because of the stages of evolution of that office, it should prove beneficial to examine the role of the governor before turning to an analysis of the discourse of women who have occupied the office. To accomplish this task, we look first to the office's historical development and then consider its modern configuration.

During colonial times, governors were considered agents of the British Crown. They enjoyed broad powers that included commanding armed forces, supervising law enforcement, convening the legislative body, vetoing legislative acts, appointing judges and officials, and granting pardons and reprieves (Rich 1–2; Lipson 9–11). After the signing of the Declaration of Independence, the former colonies rejected the colonial experience and began to form the first American state governments (Stedman 133). "The new nation's experience with colonial governors . . . became reflected in a constitutional distrust of the executive" (Rosenthal 2). Thus, the position and power of the new governorships were somewhat paltry compared to the legislature. James Madison, for instance, deemed governors "in general little more than cyphers" in comparison to the "omnipotent" legislatures (Lambert 185). Every state had some sort of executive council that "variously advised, limited, or overruled the governor" (Sabato 4). In these circumstances, governors often served as mere figureheads (Beyle 80).

Throughout the Jacksonian era, governors were hobbled because public offices were filled by popular election "and an often ill-informed electorate chose the occupants of offices that a governor should, by all administrative logic, have been able to fill by appointment" (Sabato 6). The end result was reduced power and efficiency in the state's highest office. As Sabato succinctly puts it, "[g]overnors frequently were hamstrung by the executive departments they were supposed to rule" (6). By the 1880s and 1890s, he adds, the problem had peaked as urban residents demanded an increase in state services. The governors were simply unable to control the new agencies created to serve the citizens (6).

When the Great Depression occurred, citizens perceived state governments as even less effective, for they were considered incapable of remedying the significant social ills of that era. Instead, the citizenry turned to the federal government to solve its problems, because "President Franklin D. Roosevelt captured the nation's imagination and ministered attentively to the hopes of the country" (Sabato 7). As time passed and little improvement occurred, critics of state government increased. By the late 1960s, several problems with state government were recognized publicly, including this list identified by Terry Sanford: The states are indecisive; the states are antiquated; the states are timid and ineffective; the states are not willing to face their problems; the states are not responsive; and the states have no interest in cities (1).

Laski believes that since state governments were in such sorry shape, governors were considered "second rate politicians" who merely used the governorship as a stepping-stone to a higher federal office (146). It began to look like the governorship as a political entity would deteriorate to the point of being totally ineffective and unrecognized as a force of government. However, for many reasons, the opposite occurred.

In the latter half of the twentieth century, the office of the governor has evolved into one that encompasses myriad duties and holds significant power. President Ronald Reagan's program of New Federalism, for instance, shifted the burden of providing traditional federal services to the states. Governors now must oversee an increasing array of programs and budgets. President George Bush emphasized this contemporary role of the states and their relationship to Washington at the 1989 annual meeting of the national Governors' Association. He "addressed the governors on the nation's need for educational reform, but at the same time emphasized that education was a state and local responsibility" (Rosenthal 1). In addition, using the high visibility of this office and their experience of policy formation and guidance, the most successful presidential candidates have been former governors. Jimmy Carter, Ronald Reagan, George Bush, and Bill Clinton all served as governors before becoming president. These are but two examples of how the role and power of the governorship have changed since its inception. We turn now to an examination of the modern nature of the state's highest office.

Erik B. Herzik and Brent W. Brown posit that the central figure in each state's political hierarchy is the governor (25). According to Morehouse, "the governor is at one time the head of the [political] party and the head of the government" (245). Terry Sanford delineates the powers and role of modern governors in his book, *Storm over the States.* "The governor," Sanford suggests,

by his very office embodies his state. He stands alone at his inauguration as the spokesman for all the people. . . . He must, like the President of the United States, energize his administration, search out the experts, formulate the programs, mobilize support, and carry out new ideas into action. . . . Few major undertakings ever get off the ground without his support and leadership. The governor sets the agenda for public debate; frames the issues; decides on the timing; and can blanket the state with good ideas by using his access to the mass media. . . . The governor is the most potent political power in the state. (185–188)

Clearly, then, the governor's views comprise the core of a state's policy foundation and play a pivotal role in state politics (Stedman 132).

Governors must focus on several policy concerns. One type of issue is what Herzik classifies as "perennial." These policy concerns arise every year and consist of the delivery of traditional state services such as education, highways, corrections, health care, law enforcement, and welfare (31). A second policy type that Herzik identifies is "cyclical." These are policies in which "interest grows, peaks, and then declines" (31). Policy concerns such as the environment, economic development, consumer protection, and government reorganization comprise this category (31). With Reagan's program of New Federalism, the governors' role in providing all of the above services increased dramatically.

Few of the policy concerns and services described above can become reality without a sufficient financial base. Contemporary governors in both parties maintain that fiscal responsibility is a primary key to success (Osborne 320). Not surprisingly, one of the biggest fiscal concerns facing a governor is taxes. "The vulnerability of governors," suggests Larry Sabato, is heightened by tax issues. "The vice that has squeezed so many outstanding governors," he continues, "requires more of a chief executive's time and energy and produces harried governors with less opportunity to develop a strong political base" (115).

Given the realities of state budgetary shortfalls, governors in the 1990s have faced new fiscal challenges. "Falling revenues, rising needs, a retreating national government, and desperate local governments offer them [governors] and state legislatures the responsibility for making no-win decisions: raising taxes while cutting services" (Beyle 107). Van Horn argues that governors' "survival skills are being tested as they try to meet the conflicting demands of taxpayers, recipients of government services, and interest groups" (221). Two governors discussed later in this book, Barbara Roberts and Christine Todd Whitman, found that budget cuts, taxes, and state revenues created some of the most challenging issues they encountered while in office. Roberts' situation in particular demonstrates the importance of strong leadership in times of fiscal crisis.

In order to be effective, governors must behave proactively and perform both a visionary and a managerial role in state government. Leadership qualities are key. Thad Beyle and Lynn Muchmore define the nature of this function:

The governor is looked to as an active and superior force who imposes on the far-flung bureaucracy a coherent fabric of goals and objectives and then guides the executive machinery towards these. He is more than a problem solver concerned that government functions smoothly and without corruption; he is a policy maker who sets the agenda for executive action and shapes priorities that affect decision making at every level. (82)

Much of a governor's power is derived from the perceptions that his or her citizenry holds. Governors do not have formal power over voters. However, they do possess a type of authority. That authority, Behn suggests, "comes from the state's citizens who expect the governor to solve problems, make things happen, and get the job done." If the public "genuinely expects a governor to get something done," he adds, "it will invest the governor with sufficient moral authority to see that the job is done" (55).

To achieve this moral authority, the governor must rely, in part, on personal qualities and managerial style. Cox identifies what he considers the key ingredients of a successful governor: a style that emphasizes creating change; a style that is trusting of the abilities of others; and a desire to take charge and make decisions, not as an autocrat but through and with others (59).

Clearly, for those occupying the governorship, communication skills become pivotal. Governors must be able to persuade their staff, the legislators, and their citizenry, through words and deeds, of the importance of their policies. Ultimately, suggests Larry Sabato, "an individual governor's degree of power, success, or failure will depend on his or her competence, ability, and personality" (89). As we shall see in the following chapters, women governors have used communication and managerial skills with varying degrees of success in initiating or maintaining their policies.

Since the turn of the century, only sixteen women have served as state governors. Some, like Miriam "Ma" Ferguson and Lurleen Wallace, were elected because of their husbands' political positions. Indeed, Ferguson and her husband were considered "two governors for the price of one" (Schultz 82), and she was never truly viewed as an independent thinker or leader. Table 1.1 identifies the women elected governor in the last seventy-five years, their party affiliations, states, and dates of tenure.

Although Nellie Tayloe Ross and Miriam "Ma" Ferguson were elected governors on the same day, Ross is given the honor and title of being the first woman governor because her inauguration preceded Ferguson's by two

Table 1.1
Women Governors in the United States

Governor	Party	State	Dates Served
Nellie Tayloe Ross	D	Wyoming	1925–1927
Miriam A. Ferguson	D	Texas	1925–1927; 1933–1935
Lurleen Wallace	D	Alabama	1967–1968
Ella Grasso	D	Connecticut	1975–1980
Dixie Lee Ray	D	Washington	1977–1981
Martha Layne Collins	D	Kentucky	1984–1987
Madeleine Kunin	D	Vermont	1985–1991
Kay Orr	R	Nebraska	1987–1991
Rose Mofford	D	Arizona	1988–1991
Joan Finney	D	Kansas	1991–1995
Ann Richards	D	Texas	1991–1995
Barbara Roberts	D	Oregon	1991–1995
Christine Todd Witman	R	New Jersey	1994–Present
Jeanne Shaheen	D	New Hampshire	1997–Present
Jane Dee Hull	R	Arizona	1997–Present
Nancy Hollister	R	Ohio	Dec. 31, 1998– Jan. 10, 1999

weeks. Ross accompanied her husband, an attorney, from their home in Missouri to Cheyenne as a bride in 1920. William Bradford Ross died in 1924 in the middle of a term as governor. Ross was elected to serve the remaining two years of his term and then was narrowly defeated in the next gubernatorial election (Schultz 199).

After serving her elected term as governor, Ross was elected to the Wyoming legislature. Later, she achieved national recognition in her quest to help presidential hopeful Democrat Al Smith and served as the vice-chair of the 1928 Democratic National Convention (Schultz 199). While Smith lost the election, Ross's efforts did not go unnoticed. Because of her loyalty to the party, Franklin Roosevelt appointed her director of the U.S. Mint in 1932. She retired, after 20 years of service, when Republican Dwight Eisenhower was elected president (Weatherford 301).

Miriam Amanda Wallace married Jim Ferguson on the last day of the nineteenth century. Ferguson practiced law and business and was elected governor of Texas in 1914. Because he was impeached for financial corruption in 1917, the two decided that Miriam should run for governor in 1924 to clear her husband's name. From the beginning of the campaign, "there was no doubt that she was a 'stand-in' for her husband" (Schultz 82). She acquired the nickname "Ma" during the campaign—a combination of the first letters of her first and middle names. She found the usage "distasteful" but was "smart enough to see that it was politically effective in causing voters to identify with her" (Weatherford 130).

Following her election, she worked on issues such as improvement of the education and transportation systems and "secured legislation intended to limit the Ku Klux Klan" (Weatherford 130). Publicly disagreeing with her husband, Ferguson supported prohibition and while in office advocated for tougher laws preventing the sale of liquor (Sicherman 231). After serving two nonconsecutive terms as governor, she continued to work on a progressive agenda that included aiding the poor. She died soon after the inauguration of Vice-President Lyndon B. Johnson in 1961.

It is interesting to note that the first two women governors were elected on the heels of the women's suffrage movement and that it was more than thirty years before a woman again entered the state house as governor. Although Lurleen Wallace ran an effective political campaign, she will be remembered always as the wife of George Wallace. Political analysts in Alabama posited that the electorate realized "a vote for Lurleen was a vote for George, and that George Wallace would maintain control of the state while waiting for his next opportunity to seek office" (Stineman 152). Mrs. Wallace echoed this sentiment when she said: "My election would enable my husband to carry on his programs for the people of Alabama" (qtd. in "Wallace" 449).

Lurleen Wallace had little experience in the affairs of state, except for the social spectrum of a governor's wife, and she was "shy and uneasy in public," preferring to "let her husband run the show" (Stineman 152). While campaigning, for instance, she limited her speeches to three minutes, and it is believed that it was really her husband who had penned them (Stineman 152–153). In her inaugural address, she emphasized the importance of the causes her husband had championed: segregation and opposition to forces they saw hostile to Alabama, such as China, Cuba, Russia, and Washington. In 1967, Lurleen was hospitalized with a cancerous tumor, and her husband took over all functions of running state government. When she died in 1968, the lieutenant governor assumed the governorship.

Elected governor not as the wife of an incumbent but as a candidate on her own, Ella T. Grasso had a varied political life before assuming Connecticut's highest office. Well-educated, she had received her B.A. and M.A. degrees before assuming the position of assistant director of research in Connecticut for the federal War Manpower Commission during World War II. She joined the League of Women Voters and claimed that she was "grateful to the league" because she had gained "a real understanding of issues" from her work with the organization ("Grasso" 36: 173). She began working for the Democratic Party and wrote campaign speeches, stumped for other candidates, and "chaired the Democratic State Committee for twelve years" (Schultz 98). She completed two terms in the Connecticut House of Representatives, where she introduced bills to restructure counties, reorganize the court system, and set up an office for mental retardation. During her second term, Grasso served as the assistant house leader ("Grasso" 36: 174).

In 1958, Ella Grasso was elected Connecticut's Secretary of State. She was re-elected twice and served for twelve years. She turned her office into a "people's lobby" where citizens could come to air their concerns ("Grasso" 36: 174). In the early 1970s, Grasso ran for Congress and won. She focused on education, unemployment, and minimum wage increases. Her voting record in Congress received an extremely favorable rating from liberal organizations. In 1974, she won a bid for the governorship in a landslide victory. As governor, Grasso protected the status quo and practiced frugality in state welfare and other programs. She was popular for her accessibility to voters and genuine expressions of personal concern for them ("Grasso" 43: 464). She was re-elected in 1979 but resigned in 1980 because of illness.

Governor Dixie Lee Ray of Washington had little trouble serving in a "man's" world. Indeed, during her career she was named "Maritime Man of the Year," "Man of the Year" in Seattle, and "Man of Science" by a Los Angeles science foundation. With her Ph.D. from Stanford, Ray was as comfortable in scientific circles as she was in politics. Ray directed the Pacific Science Center in Seattle and taught at the University of Washington for twenty-five years ("Ray" 55: 347). From 1973 to 1975, she served as chairperson of the Atomic Energy Commission after being appointed by President Nixon because, as she stated, "[she] was a woman" ("Ray" 34: 347). While she thrilled feminists, she angered many environmentalists with her pronuclear stance. Ray later resigned from the Atomic Energy Commission to campaign for governor.

Despite the fact that she had not run for public office before, Ray won by a wide margin. However, her term in office was marred by continuing controversy over her support for the nuclear industry and her opposition to "those environmentalists she viewed as alarmists" (Schultz 188). Ray lost the Democratic primary in 1980 in her bid for a second term in large part because of her support for increased taxation (Schultz 188).

Former Democratic National Committee Chairman Charles Manatt described Martha Layne Collins as "one of the bright new stars of our party" when she was picked to chair the National Convention of 1984 ("Collins" 91). She had worked for years as a local Democratic party volunteer in the 1960s and campaigned for Wendell H. Ford in his bid for the Kentucky governorship in 1971. Her political style was deemed "personal" and "grass roots," and she was particularly attractive to small towns and the "little man" ("Collins" 92). She held numerous statewide offices including Clerk of the Court of Appeals and Lieutenant Governor ("Ebullient Governor" 6).

In 1983, Collins mounted a fierce campaign for the office of governor and ran on a platform of crime control measures and educational improvement ("Collins" 93). She went on record as opposing abortion except in cases of rape and incest. Despite losing support from some women's groups, she beat her opponent, Republican Jim Bunning, winning 55 percent of the vote ("Collins" 93). During her term as governor, Collins sought to maintain direct lines of communication with her constituents and explained in an interview for *Christian Science Monitor* that she did "a lot of talking eyeball-to-eyeball" (qtd. in "Collins" 93). As promised in her campaign, Collins worked for educational and economic reforms during her term as governor. Like many of the women governors, Collins found herself embroiled in controversy over the issue of tax increases needed to finance the reforms she envisioned.

Madeleine Kunin began her career in local politics. In 1973, she served as a representative in Vermont's General Assembly, where she completed three terms. She received recognition for a variety of causes and became Lieutenant Governor of the state from 1979 to 1983 ("Madeleine" 1). Vermont elected her governor for three consecutive terms, from 1985 to 1991. While governor, she made sure she was accessible to the public by becoming involved in a number of civic projects. For instance, she became a commentator on Vermont Public Radio from 1991 to 1992. She founded and served as president of the board of the Institute for Sustainable Communities and was a Distinguished Visitor at Harvard's Bunting Institute. At the same time she was a Distinguished Visiting Fellow at Dartmouth College ("Madeline" 1).

During her terms as governor, Kunin eliminated a budget deficit inherited from the previous administration, increased state aid to education and child care, worked with the legislature to enact more stringent environmental laws, and established a state venture capital corporation (Mullaney 372; "Kunin" 330). A liberal Democrat, she "built a national reputation as one of the nation's most outspoken governors in the areas of abortion rights and environmental protection" (Mullaney 372). Kunin cultivated an open, consensus style of government throughout her three terms ("Kunin" 330) and appointed women to key positions in her administration (Schultz 124). Born in Zurich, Switzerland, in 1933, Ms. Kunin developed an affinity for languages and speaks German, French, and Swiss German dialect. She currently serves as the U.S. Ambassador to Switzerland.

Kay Orr of Nebraska and Rose Mofford of Arizona served in approximately the same time period. Kay Orr was the first Republican woman elected and, to date, the only woman to have faced another woman in a gubernatorial campaign ("Statewide" 1; Schultz 166). She focused on education, farming, and candidate experience during her campaign, sadly disappointing those who believed that women's issues would be emphasized. Political analysts credited Orr with being a "tough campaigner" and "hard worker" in her upset victory over her opponent (Doan and Bosc 8). Prior to being elected, Orr had spent twenty-two years working on Republican campaigns. Her previous political experience included election in 1982 to a four-year term as State Treasurer. "With that victory she became the first woman elected to a statewide constitutional office in Nebraska" (Schultz 166). Described as a "take charge governor" (Robbins A18), Orr advocated business incentives that helped lower the unemployment rate and created a sorely needed economic boom for the state. Despite these gains, Orr lost her bid for re-election in 1990 in part because a "tax-reform bill that she pushed through led to higher tax bills for nearly all Nebraskans" ("*Nebraska Politics*" 23).

Billed as the "grandmother of Arizona," a "Mae West look-alike," and "Tammy Faye Bakker in 10 years" (Foote 27), Rose Mofford served as governor after Republican Evan Mecham was impeached. A Democrat, she spent forty-seven years in state government, with posts in the offices of state treasurer and the tax commission, and she became Secretary of State in 1977 (Foote 27; Schultz 149). Political consultant Bob Jamieson says that Mofford is often misjudged because of her platinum beehive hairdo and remarks that "she is a small town personality with big time personnel and management skills" (Foote 27). She used those skills to convince the Republican-controlled legislature to sponsor a tax increase to close a state budget deficit (Toobin 13). Described as "steadfastly noncontroversial" by the *Tucson City Magazine* (qtd. in Gruson 26), Mofford chose not to run for re-election despite statewide expectations that she would ("Arizona" 24).

Ann Richards, born September 1, 1933, graduated from Waco High School in 1950. She attended Baylor University, where she majored in speech communication and minored in political science. After earning a teaching certificate from the University of Texas, she worked as a social studies and history teacher at a junior high school in Austin. Richards first entered politics in the early 1970s. She paid her Democratic Party dues by stuffing envelopes, doing grassroots campaigning, and serving as campaign manager for Sarah Weddington's 1972 state legislative race (Mullaney 359; "Richards" 469).

Richards won her first political race when she was elected county commissioner in 1976. After serving in that post for six years, she was elected as Texas State Treasurer in 1982, "becoming the first woman to hold statewide office since 'Ma' Ferguson" ("Richards" 470). While serving in this position, Richards gained fame with her now classic speech delivered at the Democratic National Convention in 1988. She then campaigned for governor that same year (Mullaney 359). Richards campaigned hard and claimed that her opponent, Clayton Williams, had "no knowledge of government" (Mullaney 361). She focused on her experience as State Treasurer. Using Populist themes, which we shall examine in an upcoming chapter, she invited voters to help her "take back government" (Mullaney 361). She went on to defeat Williams by a margin of 100,000 votes (Mullaney 361).

During her gubernatorial term, Richards "earned a reputation as a maverick for tackling stereotypically 'unfeminine' issues" (Schultz 195). She focused on improving the state economy but was unable to "make good on her no-new-taxes pledge" (Mullaney 361). Richards pushed for legislation to tighten regulations for the insurance industry and hazardous waste and promoted a new government ethics law (Mullaney 361; Schultz 195). Following her own call for a government reflective of its constituents, she "placed women and minorities in more than half of her political appointments" (Schultz 195). Despite her popularity and successful communication style, as described in chapter 5, Richards lost her bid for re-election in 1994.

A fourth-generation Oregonian, Barbara Roberts began her public service because of difficulty acquiring services for her autistic son and soon became an advocate for handicapped children. Roberts later served on local school boards, a community college board, and the Multnomah County Commission before being elected to the Oregon House of Representatives in 1981 ("Governor Barbara" 1). In 1984, she was elected Secretary of State and was re-elected to that office in 1988. Roberts ran unopposed in the Democratic primary for governor in 1990 and defeated a Republican and an Independent in the general election despite receiving less than 50 percent of the votes cast.

Roberts focused her energy on public education, human rights and services, environmental management, and streamlining state government ("Governor Barbara" 1). Her administration earned recognition for its strong gay rights advocacy, appointment of women and minorities to government positions, and support of the Oregon Health Plan ("Governor Barbara" 2). As we shall see in an upcoming chapter, the problem of insufficient state revenue created by a property tax limitation measure and failure of a state sales tax initiative consumed much of Roberts' term in office (Schultz 196). She did not seek re-election.

Born in 1925, Joan Finney began her political career as a Republican who later switched parties. She became Kansas State Treasurer in 1975 and remained in that post until her gubernatorial election in 1991. She ran in both the primary and general elections on antitax and antigovernment sentiments (Mullaney 138). Once in office, she fulfilled her pledge to veto tax increase legislation. However, she took controversial stances throughout her term and drew the criticism of feminists and pro-choice advocates for her antiabortion stance and policies (Schultz 84). She voiced her support of the militant group Operation Rescue and signed a bill into law that required parental notification for anyone under eighteen seeking an abortion and a waiting period for anyone else seeking the procedure (Mullaney 139; Schultz 84). She retired after one term in office.

Christine Todd Whitman, born in 1946, grew up in a political and financial lap of luxury. Her mother had served as the leader of the New Jersey Federation of Republican Women and as a Republican Party committeewoman. Her father, a successful building contractor and an Eisenhower appointee to economic posts in Europe, had bankrolled several Republican campaigns (Mullaney 271). In her first elected office, Christine Todd Whitman served two terms as a Somerset County freeholder and opened up the county's first homeless shelter (Mullaney 271). In 1988, she was appointed president of the State Board of Utilities, where she endeavored to keep utility rates low. She left that office in 1990 to run against Bill Bradley for the U.S. Senate. Although she was an underdog, she came within two percentage points of beating the popular incumbent.

In 1993, Whitman set her sights on the governorship and ran against Jim Florio. After a roller-coaster campaign, with polls alternately predicting victory for either candidate, she triumphed with a 25,628-vote victory, one of the smallest margins in history ("Whitman" 590) and became the first challenger "to defeat an incumbent governor in a general election in modern [New Jersey] state history" ("Christine Todd"). During her first term as governor, Whitman followed through on her promise to cut taxes by 30 percent in three years ("Whitman" 590), "enacted a 'three strikes and you're out' policy for repeat criminal offenders, and reformed welfare programs in the state" (Schultz 240). She has signed legislation creating a comprehensive school funding plan tied to statewide core curriculum standards and the bill known as "Megan's Law" ("Christine Todd"). Whitman won re-election in 1997.

Before serving in public office, Jeanne Shaheen managed several statewide campaigns, taught in public schools, and owned and managed a small business ("Jeanne" 1). New Hampshire first elected her to the State Senate in 1990. There she aimed her efforts at lowering electric rates, increasing accessibility and affordability of health care, and improving public education ("Jeanne" 1). These issues framed the core of her 1996 campaign for governor, which she won with 57 percent of the vote. While in office, Shaheen has pursued a "fiscally conservative approach to state spending while championing such causes as public kindergarten and increased tobacco taxes" (Schultz 209). She has worked to increase tourism and fund development of new businesses. In addition, she has supported legislation to stabilize health insurance rates, eliminate discrimination against people with preexisting conditions, and provide protections for HMO consumers ("Jeanne" 1). In June 1997, Shaheen approved a law protecting lesbians and gay men against discrimination ("New Hampshire Chief" 37). Re-elected in 1998, she continues her fight to lower New Hampshire's electric utility rates.

Prior to her service as Arizona's highest elected official, Jane Dee Hull was elected as the first Republican Secretary of State in 1995. She served in the Arizona House of Representatives from 1979 to 1983, where she held several committee and leadership positions, including a term as Majority Whip and two terms, from 1989 to 1992, as the first woman elected Speaker of the House ("Governor Jane" 1). Hull began her political career in 1965 as Republican precinct committeewoman and deputy registrar. She also chaired several high-profile Republican campaigns ("Governor Jane" 1).

Hull became governor through constitutional succession in September 1997, when Governor Fife Symington was convicted of fraud and resigned from office (Greenblatt 2094). She won election in her own right in the 1998 gubernatorial campaign ("Statewide" 1). "As governor, Hull has made education, children, preserving Arizona's natural beauty and the economy her top priorities ("Governor Jane" 1).

Lieutenant governor Nancy Hollister became Governor of Ohio when her predecessor, George Voinovich, stepped down to take the U.S. Senate seat he had won in the November 1998 election ("Statewide" 1). Sworn in on December 31, 1998, she served as governor for eleven days. Hollister began her political career in 1980, when she won a seat on the Marietta City Council. Her career at the local level culminated in a four-year term as mayor of Marietta. In 1991, Governor Voinovich "tapped her to manage the Governor's Office of Appalachia" ("Gov. Hollister" 2).

Hollister was elected as Ohio's first woman Lieutenant Governor in 1994 (Jacobs 1). During her tenure in that office, she oversaw the Ohio Bureau of Employment Services, the Ohio Department of Agriculture, and the Ohio Coal Development Office ("Gov. Hollister" 10A). "She was the chief architect of Jobs Bill III, an economic stimulus package aimed at Ohio's distressed urban and rural communities" ("Gov. Hollister" 2). Hollister's principal action during her term as governor was the signing of a bill creating agricultural easements for farmland preservation. She was involved in the creation of this bill as cochair of the Ohio Farmland Preservation Task Force in 1997 (Chorpening 6B). Following her stint as governor, she was appointed to fill a vacant seat in the Ohio House of Representatives and now serves as the representative from the 96th District (Leonard 5B).

Given the impressive credentials of these sixteen women, we may ask why so few other women have sought or been elected to their states' highest office. Susan Carroll contends that political opportunity variables such as, "objective aspects of the political situation not subject to direct control by the individual politician" create "impediments to increasing the numbers of women holding public office" (158). She suggests that "barriers in the political opportunity structure affect the recruitment of women candidates, reduce their probability of winning election, and constrain their future officeholding aspirations" (158). Nancy McGlen and Karen O'Connor identify five interrelated barriers that prevent women from gaining political office. These include stereotypes, career choice and preparation, family demands, sex discrimination, and the political system (95). They note that "barriers to political activity, while diminished since 1920, can still be formidable" and that "system-level barriers, especially those that favor incumbents, make it difficult for women to reach parity" in political participation (95).

As McGlen and O'Connor allege, negative attitudes and stereotypes have served to hinder women's ascent to the governorship. And, as Dianne Feinstein argues, "it is clearly more difficult for women to succeed in politics," for they "have to prove themselves effective and credible time and time again" (qtd. in Cantor and Bernay xv). Furthermore, politics and political behavior often are seen as masculine endeavors, and therefore, it is believed that women have no place in the political arena (Cantor and Bernay 7). Echoing this idea, Barbara Roberts notes that "it's harder for a woman generally to raise large amounts of money and be a major candidate for a major office"(Guttman 30). Finally, few women have become governors because in some party circles they are viewed still as "reserve" candidates "who deserve to carry the banner only in hopeless elections, as did Republican gubernatorial candidates Louise Gore of Maryland and Shirley Crumplext of Nevada in 1974" (Sabato 24). Many of these barriers to women's participation in the political arena are discussed in more detail in subsequent chapters.

Despite these obstacles, women are beginning to enter the political arena in more than token numbers. As Dianne Feinstein points out, women "begin at the local level, perhaps on a school board, city council, board of supervisors, or a legislator's campaign staff or government agency" (qtd. in Canton and Bernay xv). Women then work their way up the political ladder. Since "state legislative and executive offices are the traditional staging areas for campaigns for statewide and federal positions," more women can be expected to run for a higher office, such as governor, in the future (Cantor and Bernay 7).

The increasing importance of the state governor throughout the history of the country, coupled with women's steadily expanding role in that office, demonstrates that the face of the governorship *has* changed. The women discussed in the following chapters have helped redefine the nature and role of the governorship. Each woman encountered a plethora of obstacles and navigated boundaries to forge her own unique path while seeking or maintaining this position. As the number of women holding their state's highest office increases, so too does the need for research in this previously neglected area of women's political communication. In this spirit, we offer the following chapters not merely as critical analysis but as a starting point for crucial discussion.

Chapter Two

Marginalizing Metaphors of the Feminine

Kristina Horn Sheeler

Women governors in the United States find themselves contained within an articulation of liberal democracy that, since the country's founding, has associated executive leadership with distinctly masculine traits. As Georgia Duerst-Lahti and Rita Mae Kelly explain, women enter the realm of public leadership "within ideological terms of masculine norms" (20). Even though men and women gain access to political leadership, their access is different and shaped in masculine terms. Women must negotiate a liberal democratic political culture in which liberalism's masculine control over democracy conceives of democracy simultaneously as a weak and fragile entity (as feminine) and as a rhetorical stylistics causing a decline in civic discourse. Furthermore, as it is currently sutured, liberal democracy justifies militarism over feminine inclusion and gender diversity. As a result, women executives risk becoming politically marginalized by the reified metaphor of masculine rationality that defines democratic deliberation and frames daily news coverage of political events, practices, and personae.

These assumptions play out specifically in the ways that women governors are characterized. To date, our country has elected or appointed sixteen women to the position of state governor. While more women have risen to the ranks of Congress, none functions with the individual executive power afforded to the position of governor. Yet, while increasing numbers of women are filling representative positions, women in gubernatorial positions are not growing as steadily. Several scholars and political analysts suggest that we may be more likely to accept "women who represent us" than women who take charge and run things on their own (Tolleson-Rinehart and Stanley 3). It follows that for women, the role of representing is less a violation of the masculine liberal democratic political culture than the role of leading. After all, leading requires aggression, initiative, expertise, and reason. Representing requires concern and deference to the public good, connection, and concern for humane rather than personal interests. This makes the sixteen women who have occupied the governor's mansion an interesting study in the characterizations of leadership. Some of these women have made an impact not only on the state level but on the national level as well, suggesting that they may be able to affect leadership culture just as productively on a larger scale.

If we are somehow more comfortable with women who represent us rather than those who run things on their own, what does this say about the characterization of leadership in general—and the governorship in particular? In the words of Molly Ivins, a Texas journalist asked to contemplate whether a woman could handle the position of governor, "Think of the amount of cultural expectation attached to a title like 'Governor.' And what you invariably get is the tall, distinguished, white-haired man" (qtd. in Tolleson-Rinehart and Stanley 57). If this is the case, then there are serious implications for women. Feminist scholars point out that when women public officials attempt to negotiate the prevailing political ideology, they are more likely regarded as lacking, deficient, or somehow inappropriate (Duerst-Lahti and Kelly 19), in part because our culture has constructed *woman* as feminine and separate from the rational political sphere in which political deliberation supposedly takes place. The result is to literalize rather than question the underlying gender constructions of political practice and their implications for women seeking political office.

Based on a survey of all sixteen women governors, beginning with media representations of Nellie Tayloe Ross in 1925 through 1927, I have identified four clusters of metaphors existing in newspaper and magazine characterizations of women elected to the governorship: pioneer, puppet, beauty queen, and unruly woman. While not a definitive survey of all media, this survey considers major publications with large national audiences such as the Associated Press Political Service, the *New York Times*, *Newsweek*, *Time*, and the *Nation* as well as local, historical, and women's magazines such as *Current Opinion*, the *Literary Digest*, and the *Woman Citizen*. My analysis of these sources included the years just prior to and including each woman governor's term in office. My survey of these sources was thorough to the point of being indicative of the main metaphorical patterns used to characterize women executives, defining public perceptions of leadership and undermining the work that women do as leaders.

As Kenneth Burke explains, metaphoric clusters are terms that evoke similar rhetorical motives (*Attitudes* 232–234). Metaphors and their corresponding motives provide a fertile foundation for a study of women governors in order to assess the constraints placed upon them by liberal democracy's patriarchal impulses. Women leaders do not simply appear on the scene but appear among a complex set of images and expectations that has evolved as our country has elected and will continue to elect women public officials. The prevailing metaphors are significant in that they frame expectations concerning what is appropriate for public officeholders who are women and the impact they may have on leadership culture. Furthermore, the metaphors themselves are problematic for thinking about women in positions of leadership and should compel critics and public officials alike to undertake the productive work of transforming such restrictive imagery.

GOVERNOR AS PIONEER

The first and probably most obvious metaphoric cluster used to characterize women in the position of governor is "pioneer." A pioneer is someone who is a trailblazer or groundbreaker in the sense that most of these women were the first elected woman governor of their state and have many other "firsts" lining their biographies. Their determination, practical wisdom, perseverance, and hard work characterize pioneers. Miriam Ferguson, for example, was called "a stalwart, this pioneer woman Governor-in-prospect" after her successful run in the Democratic primary ("Miriam" 436), and the *Literary Digest* of November 1924 claimed that the pioneering efforts of Ross and Ferguson certainly meant that "women have taken a step toward the White House," smoothing the way remarkably for women ("Woman's" 17).

Similarly, one of Dixy Lee Ray's advisers likened her campaign to a Lewis and Clark expedition (Chu 47), and in Ella Grasso's obituary, her husband is quoted, calling Grasso " 'a pioneer. If she succeeds, she makes it easier for thousands of women in future generations.' Succeed she did" ("Connecticut's" 20). Even Christine Todd Whitman's pioneering qualities were used to encourage her to run for the vice-presidency, where she could do the same pioneering work she is doing in the governorship, and Bob Dole notes her "virtually unlimited potential" (Ayres 37).

Pioneers are also known for their "pioneering spirit," a quality appealing to "common folks" working hard side by side, demonstrating that you do not have to be exceptional to possess pioneering qualities and underscoring the "grassroots" attraction of many of these women. In particular, this spirit is reminiscent of the populist rhetoric of the late nineteenth century that beckoned to the honest laborer who had been "forgotten" by the government. This spirit was especially evident in the characterizations of western and southwestern women of Texas, Wyoming, Kansas, and Nebraska. The *Nation* explained "Ma" Ferguson's appeal to "common folks" and called the Fergusons "self styled champions of the forgotten man" (Preece 255). Following Ross's election, the *Woman Citizen* claimed that she was "devoted to the rights of the common people" ("Women" 9) and in March 1925 called her a "well-rounded, able and engaging woman" after her attendance at the presidential inauguration (Stokes 8). In commenting upon the ability of Wyoming women to handle themselves with political responsibilities such as suffrage, Elizabeth Stokes proceeded to explain: "Hardy and intelligent women in the old days came to Wyoming and pitched in with the men" (8).

The pioneering spirit of the women governors enabled them to appeal to the "common people," "the forgotten man." Nancy Bocskor, Nebraska's Republican Party executive director, explained that the woman-versus-woman 1986 gubernatorial race in Nebraska had come about because of the state's "pioneer spirit—women and men working hard side by side" (qtd. in Doan and Bosc 8). Joan Finney, the first woman governor of Kansas, "attributed her victory to having drawn on her own reservoir of goodwill . . . by espousing populist ideas . . . giving the people more control" ("Joan" 1). Her "grassroots support" was credited with upsetting her opponent (1).

The grassroots appeal of these pioneering politicians allowed them in some cases to distance themselves from the woman question and later feminism, since feminism was characterized as radical, aggressive, and extreme—not mainstream or the focus of common, hard-working folks. Ferguson insisted she ran for governor for her husband's sake and not to advance women's issues. When asked if she had any advice for women, she responded, " 'Why certainly not! Why should I?' in plain surprise" (Bentley 12). Ella Grasso of Connecticut downplayed the feminist issue, calling herself "just an old shoe" (qtd. "Grasso: Piedmont" 10), and Dixy Ray of Washington State demanded to be called Chairman of the Atomic Energy Commission, not Chairperson, insisting she was not a "feminist crusader—'I'm not a joiner type' " ("Dixy Rocks" 31).

However, because there are only sixteen women who have served as governors, their pioneering achievements can easily be chalked up to their status as symbolic rather than serious leaders. The *Progressive* considered Ella Grasso "symbolic of what the American Woman could achieve through hard work, perseverance, intelligence, and political toughness rather than through sexuality and appeals to the male sense of justice. Her symbolic position has not changed. But the question is whether she has the courage and the ability to be a first-rate governor" (Burnham, "Testing" 34). Madeleine Kunin of Vermont was up-front about the "symbolic element to her campaign": " 'Let's face it, I'm charting a new course,' Kunin says. 'So far there are no portraits in the statehouse which look like mine' " ("Vermont" 44). Even the *Woman Citizen* pointed out that the achievements of Ross and Ferguson may have been remarkable, but "neither case is an all-wool feminist triumph" since neither succeeded "wholly on [her] own records" ("Women" 9). They were merely anomalies, "unusual" achievements ("Women" 9), the exception that proved the rule. Thus, while these pioneering women could be congratulated, there is also an underlying skepticism of their abilities to govern successfully until such time as they are able to prove themselves. Once again, women are easily marginalized because they are symbolic, not serious or courageous leaders. They may work hard, but often beside men, not on their own. Just as the rational norms of the political culture are suspicious of rhetoric, these norms are also suspicious of women's achievements, causing their capability as executive leaders to be dismissed and further reifying the patriarchal expectations of the political sphere.

GOVERNOR AS PUPPET

Women governors will not be able to prove themselves while they are considered puppets. The puppet is the most passive of the metaphoric clusters and is exemplified in Governors Miriam "Ma" Ferguson of Texas and Lurleen Wallace of Alabama. Both Ferguson and Wallace ran for governor because their husbands could not. Jim Ferguson had been impeached in 1917 in Texas, and George Wallace could not run for a consecutive term in Alabama in 1966. Many sources were very direct when reporting this situation. For example, the *Outlook* explained that "Mrs. Ferguson was selected to run . . . not as a woman, but as a wife. Her supporters would have chosen her husband . . . if they could" (" 'Me' " 5). A caption at the beginning of an article in the *Saturday Evening Post* declared that "Wallace is running in his wife's name" (Harold Martin 25). However, Wallace assured the voters there would be no "petticoat government. If [Lurleen] were elected she would be governor in name only. He would run the state as he always had" (26).

The governor as puppet is an instrument, an object, a token to be manipulated by some more powerful other—most often a man, and more specifically a husband. This is most clearly demonstrated by a cartoon in *Collier's* of April 1926 depicting "Pa" seated and a little "Ma" on his lap with Pa moving her mouth ("Petticoat" 19). The caption read, "Now sing us a little song," and the article itself suggested Ferguson had acted "merely as the puppet" of a man. "When anybody calls at the governor's office, he must see GOVERNOR Jim first. And Mrs. Ferguson cannot open her mouth until he speaks. He is the ventriloquist, and she is the dummy. She admits it" ("Petticoat" 19). Not only was Mrs. Ferguson apparently a ventriloquist's dummy, but she was also "the only weapon" that Texas voters "could put their hands on" to defeat the Ku Klux Klan (Field 554). In other words, she would do. The article continued by stating that the voters of Texas "gave no thought to the quality or merit of the weapon employed, reasoning that in two years they could dispose of Mrs. Ferguson and supplant her with a more worthy instrument" (555). Clearly, Ferguson did not win the election so much as the Ku Klux Klan lost. At best, her admission to the governorship was passive, fitting for a woman. She gave "little distinction to the office" she held (555).

Without the aid of a cartoon, Lurleen Wallace was aptly depicted as a showpiece that her husband could wield from town to town in *his* re-election bid. An article in the *Atlantic Monthly* of August 1967 began:

Through the spring and fall campaigns last year, she tagged after him as he scuttled, with the tense urgency of a squirrel, across the map of Alabama. They put her, with one female companion, in a separate car behind his, and she was reverently borne from town to town like some irreplaceable ceremonial fixture, a token to lend the dubious enterprise a measure of legitimacy and sanction. . . . She submitted to it with an air composed, patient, somewhat inert and remote—a small, quiet figure, smiling pleasantly and a little uneasily, with an expression sometimes, as she squinted in the sun, faintly perplexed. (Frady 35)

Clearly, Lurleen Wallace was considered George's token to show from town to town, often called his "proxy" ("In" 39), "a distinctive footnote," his "appendage" (Margolick 16), and described in passive terms, all appropriate characterizations of a woman in patriarchal leadership culture.

At best, the governor as puppet is simply "a stand-in," "proxy," "surrogate," or "follower," dutifully submitting to the husband who put her there. The implication is that there are appropriate and natural roles for women in relation to men, specifically their husband; and more importantly, the role of governor comes in direct opposition to the role of wife. Thus, wife must take precedence over politician, allowing a woman to maintain her proper subservient role.

In an article titled "Can a Wife Be Governor?" *Collier's* drew the distinction between Ma Ferguson's marriage vow "to love, cherish and to OBEY" her husband and the oath that she took as governor to "faithfully and impartially discharge and perform all the duties incumbent upon me as governor of Texas" (W. Whitman 5). According to *Collier*'s, "If she turns a deaf ear to reform measures and the pleas of other women, she does it not as a traitor to the cause of women's rights, which she never espoused, but in traditional feminine loyalty to one man" (W. Whitman 6). And so in running for governor she obeyed her husband. "Only as a matter of wifely duty does Miriam A. Ferguson serve her term, a political prisoner in her own office" (W. Whitman 6). If she wanted to act on her own, she could not, *Collier*'s pointed out; "she'd just break up her home" (6). Furthermore, the Norfolk *Virginian-Pilot* suggested that the puppet imagery undermined any power that women governors may gain through simultaneous characterization as a pioneer. Ferguson's "apparent surrender of power to her husband dims the luster of Mrs. Ferguson's accomplishment as one of the women pioneers in State politics" ("Is Pa" 15). The metaphoric clusters characterizing women in politics simultaneously keep women in their proper place and reinforce the masculine rational norms of control that have long characterized domestic politics.

Many of the women governors had to contend with similar criticisms. For example, Ella Grasso, often called the first woman governor who did not follow in her husband's footsteps, had to battle criticisms that she was not a serious governor. When her legislature passed a budget despite her warnings that it could create a huge debt for Connecticut and then she refused to veto or amend it, the media labeled her "an 'invisible governor,' who was 'governing by default' and 'playing politics' by setting up members of her own party for attack in the 1978 elections" (Burnham, "Governor" 36). *Newsweek* claimed that Ann Richards was selected to deliver the keynote address at the 1988 Democratic convention simply "to score points in the South and to exploit George Bush's gender-gap woes" (Pedersen 22). And, according to the *New York Times*, Whitman had to contend with "persistent rumors" that her husband had "undue influence" over her policy decisions and her campaigns (Pulley B1). Whitman also had to deal with attacks that she was simply a token woman delivering the response to the president's 1995 State of the Union address. Jay Severin, a Republican consultant, acknowledged: "If she were Christopher Whitman and not Christie Whitman, she wouldn't be giving the response" (qtd. in "Christine Whitman" 2). It is not uncommon for women governors to have to contend with criticisms undermining their political clout or leadership ability and suggesting that they are merely tokens to be used by their parties. These images keep gender relations in check while they also dismiss any rhetorical sensitivity on the part of women governors who attempt to negotiate the prevailing masculine political norms. As a result, women and rhetoric continue to be marginalized as serious contributors to liberal democratic politics.

GOVERNOR AS BEAUTY QUEEN

The governor-as-puppet cluster suggests that there is a proper role for women in relation to men. They are invisible, follow behind, and are available to be used and manipulated for whatever cause. If women are to become public figures, then how might they do so? One avenue is seemingly to praise women for their "proper talents," thus leading to characterizations of women governors as "beauty queens" and continuing to keep gender relations in bounds. The governor-as-beauty queen concept encapsulates a cluster of metaphors representing all things for which traditional women are allowed praise in public: They are sometimes giddy, attractive social creatures who win popularity contests and enjoy playing hostess and caretaker. Martha Layne Collins exemplifies this metaphor of governor-as-beauty queen, being a former Kentucky Derby ceremonies queen herself. While this metaphoric cluster appears to allow women a more active role than governor-as-puppet does, it still underscores women's femininity and attention to beauty and appearance as appropriate and reinscribes women's traditional role in a hierarchical family structure. These are the reasons for her appeal. The rhetorical sensitivity that goes along with playing hostess, for example, is completely overlooked. As Martha Layne Collins will admit, she poured many cups of coffee and hosted many dinners to get to the governor's mansion.

Consider this description of Nellie Tayloe Ross, our country's first "Governor Lady" ("Governor Lady" 67), a title noting her proper upbringing, regarding her attendance at the presidential inaugural in 1925: "Governor Ross delighted the capital. Her poise was excellent, her appearance splendid, her stories good, and her speeches modest but full of fact as well as spirit. . . . A medium-sized, pleasant, smiling, youthful woman with a delightful voice in which there were tones of restraint, authority and geniality—and a good-looking face with soft lines" (Stokes 8). This sounds like the description of the Miss America pageant winner: excelling in poise, beauty, speaking, and congeniality.

The connection is much more direct with Martha Layne Collins, who was compared with the outgoing Kentucky governor's wife, Phyllis George, a former beauty pageant winner herself: "The two women have much in common. Both were reared in small towns and influenced by strong mothers. Both became cheerleaders, sorority members and beauty queens," but unlike George, Collins "sometimes wears homemade clothes and buys off the rack" and often does her own hair (Rozen and Brecher 59). "She backed the Equal Rights Amendment but has done little for it." (59) Former FDR adviser Edward Prichard claimed "She doesn't threaten any-one. Small-town women like her and men think she looks like a nice wife and mother" (qtd. In Rozen and Brecher 59). She and her husband also en-joy entertaining. According to a friend, "If you don't let her wait on you, she won't be happy" (60).

Collins described her gubernatorial duties as "the state's official hostess" (qtd. in Sirotu 109). She explained her entertaining hints, such as choosing flowers, and "her formula of making each event special" (109). She likes "simplicity and elegance—nothing too showy or intimidating" when plan-ning and has a tradition of "presenting each guest with a party favor at meal's end" (110). She encourages "all hostesses [to] nurture their creative spirit" and includes a few of her favorite recipes for Kentucky Quiche, Cheese Grits, and Cinnamony Fried Apples (110).

As long as the woman governor is a beautiful hostess and entertainer, she upholds the traditional feminine expectations of her gender role. We are not forced to reconsider what it means to be a woman in a position of leader-ship—allowing masculinity to become reinscribed as the norm. Addi-tionally, the antirhetorical nature of the political sphere ignores the leadership activities that go into planning a dinner party and playing host-ess.

Neither did the giddy beauty queen image bypass Madeleine Kunin: "In the cramped back seat of what passed in unpretentious Vermont for an offi-cial limousine sat slender, blue-eyed, 51-year-old Madeleine Kunin, who giggled. 'Isn't this fun?' she whispered to a companion. 'You have to re-member this is still a bit new to me' " (Runnion 105). After she replaced Vermont's agricultural commissioner with an appointment of her own, she commented, "I felt like such a meanie" (qtd. in Runnion 105).

Also, Kunin was presented as a hostess in *McCall's*, introducing readers to some " 'very Vermont' delicacies" (Rossant 82). Perhaps in an effort to upstage her "aggressive," "hardball" image ("Second" 31; "Vermont" 42), Kunin the hostess opened her own door to greet journalists; she served cof-fee in a room that was "warm and informal (just like the governor)"; she was called by her first name (Rossant 82). She balances her time between offi-cial duties, family, and friends, and "does make sure to gather with her friends over coffee and maple upside-down cake [recipe included] at least once a month" (Rossant 83). She likes cooking with Vermont produce and was pictured with "some of her favorite cooking utensils" (83).

The beauty queen prepares for public office through traditional means: She is a schoolteacher and homemaker, or if in public, the Secretary of

State, which is traditionally a woman's office. The *Literary Digest* quoted Arthur Rex Graham, a Consolidated Press Association correspondent: "Mrs. Ross yet is the perfect type of homemaker. She plans to 'keep house' for the State as she did for William Ross, practising [*sic*] the homely virtues of rigid economy, neatness, orderliness and efficiency" ("Wyoming's" 13), and quoted the Birmingham *News*: "The majority of women being natural-born housekeepers, why shouldn't the infinite detail of a Governor's office appeal to the female of the species? . . . [E]very woman who ever filled her job fully as head of a home has had excellent training to be Mayor and Governor" ("Woman's" 17). An Associated Press Candidate Bio profiled Collins as "a former teacher and beauty queen" ("Martha" 1); Jane Hull of Arizona was "a fiscally conservative former schoolteacher" (Purdum 20), and Rose Mofford also of Arizona was a lifetime "state employee who took a caretaker approach" (Purdum 20). An Associated Press Candidate Bio on Jane Hull further highlighted her elementary education degree and public school teaching experience ("Jane" 1), and Jeanne Shaheen was identified as a high school teacher and "consensus-builder" ("Cynthia" 1).

In the beauty queen we have the traditional stereotypical woman, a beautiful mother and hostess who is active in public within certain parameters. What is evident in many of the descriptors of the beauty queen is the obsessive focus on appearance, clearly reinforcing the myth that to be valued, a woman must be beautiful. Additionally, beauty and leadership are seen as dichotomous terms. The beautiful woman can never be trusted, for she will arouse the passions, not the intellect, of those around her, or she is too irrational herself. Also, a woman is more often at home dealing with children as a teacher or caretaker, not a leader who deals with adults. The metaphorical imagery creates a suspicion of the feminine, the passions, and rhetoric and underscores women's proper role in the family, reinforcing the masculine rational norms of political culture.

GOVERNOR AS UNRULY WOMAN

Focus on appearance carries over into the fourth, and final, cluster of metaphors. Whereas the beauty queen is beautiful, the fourth cluster emphasizes reversal, pointing out how some women governors simply do not measure up in the poise-and-appearance category. The final cluster is also the most complex and significant, for successful management contributes to the leadership successes of recent women governors. It incorporates a range of gendered images emphasizing disruption, dichotomy, and reversal, and often reversal of the beauty queen cluster's emphasis on appearance and family structure. This reversal ranges from the masculine, "bitchy" Dixy

Lee Ray to "female governor" Kay Orr, who was elected governor while her husband stayed home to bake meat loaf and write cookbooks. Additionally, the reversal creates the sense that the woman elected to the masculine office is somehow unfitting, disorienting, the butt of humor, or just an unlikely candidate for the position.

The juxtaposition accomplishes a variety of purposes. It may be to point out the lack of a necessary feminine quality in a biologically sexed female who has allowed the masculine to overcharacterize her—perhaps a woman is "bitchy," a political "maverick." Or, it may be to provide the appearance of balance for political actions required by the situation—perhaps a woman is fulfilling the masculine expectations of leader, but she is also compassionate and caring, doing her job as woman. Yet, the result is dichotomous thinking in which gendered terms are seen as opposites that do not fit together or fit together awkwardly. Or, it may be to emphasize an inappropriate or comical relationship between the governor and her "First Man," created as a result of the woman's election to public office. Whatever the gendered incongruity, the characterization of the woman official is seen as strange, humorous, ungenuine, and especially disruptive to the social hierarchy, and it ultimately undermines the power and authority of the woman governor who is not following the prescribed, antirhetorical expectations of the masculine political sphere.

This cluster, in which gender construction and reversal are at issue, encompasses what Kathleen Rowe calls the "Unruly Woman." According to Rowe, the unruly woman is found in a range of examples from Mae West, Barbara Stanwyck, and Katharine Hepburn to Miss Piggy and Roseanne Barr. More important, the unruly woman opens the possibility for "recoding and reauthoring the notion of 'Woman' " (Rowe 31). The unruly woman creates a spectacle of herself, emphasizing the social construction of gender. In addition, the unruly woman

1. creates disorder by dominating, or trying to dominate, men. She will not confine herself to her proper place.
2. is excessive physically, she may be fat, and excessive in speech, in quantity, content, or tone.
3. makes jokes, or laughs herself.
4. may be old or a masculinized crone.
5. is associated with thresholds, borders, or margins, and taboo. (Rowe 31)

These characteristics result when women disrupt the expectations of femininity and the social hierarchy. Even though the governor as unruly woman disrupts boundaries, the metaphor also tells us that the woman has transgressed. Such a spectacle becomes problematic when thinking about women public officials, unless the woman can find a way to use it to her advantage to advance a more productive metaphor.

Two governors exemplify this cluster: Dixy Lee Ray and Kay Orr. Ray is the bitchy extreme, overly masculine, while Orr has apparently switched gender roles with her husband, causing a concern about his masculinity. As a result, descriptions of Ray focus on her inappropriately unfeminine, radical qualities that somehow make her less of a woman, and by extension an inappropriate, eccentric governor. Descriptions of Orr focus on her husband, attempting to give him a voice that justifies his nontraditional gender role.

Ray was a well-educated woman, yet media descriptions often put her education secondary: "Dr. Ray, who is single, has degrees in zoology and biology" ("AEC" 17). Other descriptions note: "Ray, who never married, lives with her sister" (Keerdoja 16). *Time* claimed, "Her manner is brisk and candid. Her taste in clothes runs to blazers and tweed skirts with knee socks and 'sensible' shoes. A sturdy, affable spinster of 59, Dixy Lee Ray lives in an 8–ft.-by-28–ft. motor home" (Iker 98). Even in her obituary, the *Los Angeles Times* described her as "a short, chunky woman with cropped hair and tailored clothes. . . . she was called Dick as a child—short for 'that little Dickens'" and later changed her name to Dixy Lee, "after a favorite region and a Civil War General" ("Dixy Lee" 3).

Newsweek encompassed many of the image issues leveled at Ray: "the major newspapers opposed her, her foes chuckled and just about everyone predicted the state was not ready for an unmarried woman who gave herself a chain saw for Christmas" (Mathews 45). She lived in the governor's mansion with her sister and had a very straightforward style, firing all appointees of the previous governor. As Ray stated, "So I said if they needed it, I'd send them a box of Kleenex—along with their pink slip" (qtd. in Mathews 45). *Newsweek* continued to describe her as "a short woman with gray hair, plump, rosy cheeks, an engaging smile—and a sharp wit." She "has no real program of her own" and "pads around the governor's mansion in Hush Puppies and keeps her poodle, Jacques, at her feet under her desk in the governor's office" (Mathews 45). As Ray countered, "If I don't conform to the image of what a governor should be or act like, I'm sorry. . . . But I'm not going to spend hours agonizing over it. I grew up before self-analysis became a popular indoor sport" (qtd. in Mathews 45).

Ray's political approach was considered "maverick" ("Surprises" 45; "Dixy Rocks" 27, 31). She had "the subtlety of a Seattle stevedore" who doesn't walk but "stalks" or "bulldozes" (Chu 47; "Dixy Rocks" 26). Yet, she was described with a warm side: "radiat[ing] a charm that makes her seem like a benevolent pixie, a chubby (5 ft. 4 in., 165 lbs.) Peter Pan" ("Dixy Rocks" 27). "She has a streak of Golda Meir in her," according to a former Atomic Energy Commission member, and her aides were intimidated by her and named "yes-yes-yes people" ("Dixy Rocks" 31). Her opponents promoted bumper stickers saying "Ditch the Bitch," and her 1976 campaign manager claimed she had a "highhanded style," that "ridiculed" and "antagonized people" (Williams 28; "Defeat" 25). As a *Time* article concluded: "Dixy Lee Ray relishes too much delivering thunderbolts from the Olympia of her own Washington" ("Dixy Rocks" 35).

The other prototype of this final cluster is Kay Orr. Orr is not the bitchy, overly masculinized leader, but it is clear that with a woman in a leadership position, there is also a problem concerning who wears the pants in the family. The focus of her characterizations is on the disruption that her position creates within her family structure; however, it is cast as humorous and as something one would find in a sitcom. It is certainly not something to see in the world of politics. Furthermore, the reversal casts her husband in the starring role because of his identity crisis and paints the governor as a "female" governor so that she does not appear overly masculine and as a result efface her husband's masculinity.

The following headline encapsulated the problem: "While Nebraska Governor Kay Orr Makes Policy, Husband Bill, Her 'First Gentleman,' Bakes Meat Loaf" (Kaufman and Mills 189). The article proceeded:

It sounds like the premise for a sitcom: When his wife becomes Governor of a midwestern state, a hotshot insurance executive has to find ways of coping on the home front. Forthcoming episodes deal with husband learning to cook, husband (henceforth to be known as First Gentleman) being seated with the wives at the Governors' conference, and husband deploring the décor of the Governor's mansion.

Turn off the laugh track, folks, this is no sitcom. It's the very happy real-life story of Nebraska's first female Governor. . . . Her husband . . . suddenly had to worry about the house while Kay worried about the senate. (Kaufman and Mills 189)

The article explained that Orr's transformation began when Kay became state treasurer and "housekeeping would have to be an either Orr proposition." Kay said that she "taught Bill that being patient and understanding about my job was not simply waiting for me to come home and fix his meal. . . . That was very nice of him, but he had to take it one step further and fix himself his own meal" (qtd. in Kaufman and Mills 189, 191). Bill finds he is a veteran meat loaf maker and "is comfortable with the role of consort and official spouse" (191). Bill and Madeleine Kunin's husband "seek each other out at gubernatorial gatherings. 'We sit in the back corner and talk. . . . Sometimes they have to shush us' " (192). Bill also put together *The*

First Gentleman's *Cookbook* and used the royalties from the book to reno-
vate the governor's mansion, previously decorated in "early Holiday Inn,"
according to Mr. Orr (Kaufman and Mills 192).

The Lincoln *Journal* also captured this odd reversal, praising Mr. Orr's
good sense of humor as he defined "how the state's First Man should act"
(qtd. in Schmidt 14). Orr responded that he has a good sense of humor and
that he has "nothing to be embarrassed about here. I'm just as proud as I can
be about my wife" (14). He admitted that "he has taken his share of ribbing"
about being the "First Man"—his friend told him he should change his
name to Adam. Another friend called him "The Governor's Bagman" when
a picture of Bill holding Kay's purse ran in newspapers (14).

Such concern over the apparent masculinity of a husband or a state that
would elect a woman governor was even expressed with Miriam Ferguson's
election in 1925 with a cartoon depicting a very small Texas tied to a very
large Ma's apron strings ("Texas" 11). Additionally, Shana Alexander writing in *Life* magazine likened the 1966 Alabama gubernatorial election to Al
Capp's "Li'l Abner" comic strip. As Alexander wrote: "When Governor
Wallace said Lurleen was to be the candidate, a Southern newspaper commented, 'It's as difficult to imagine her running for governor as it is to imagine Helen Hayes butchering a hog.' Not, evidently, for the people of
Alabama. And not for us *Li'l Abner* fans, either" (19).

Exaggerating the incongruity between traditional gender roles and their
reversal focuses attention on gender's construction while it also disrupts the
social hierarchy. What we are left with is trying to make sense of women
leaders using dichotomies that can be equally as problematic since they are
rooted in mutually exclusive expectations. The *Atlantic Monthly* described
Lurleen Wallace as: "A small tidy woman with a fondness for blazers and
turtleneck blouses, which make her look like the leader of a girls' college
glee club, she is attractive in that hard, plain, small-faced somewhat masculine way that Deep Southern women tend to be attractive—in fact, over the
years, she has even acquired a certain resemblance to her husband" (Frady
37). Bringing together oppositional terms serves only to make the woman
governor appear unnatural or ungenuine, reinforcing the norm that she is
acting outside appropriate borders and that her behaviors are unruly and
taboo.

Newsweek pointed out Ella Grasso's "cropped brown hair is frequently a
mess," her spectacles are frequently on her head, and her "baggy beige pant-
suit . . . [and] lace-up shoes" contribute to her "rumpled image" in which she
"looks as if she was left behind by a tornado" ("On the Run" 21). This article
goes on to note: "the larger irony is that Grasso, 55, happens to be a woman
much as Babe Ruth happened to have spindly legs; it is a minor but much

dwelt-upon characteristic that sometimes obscures the true stamp of a tough, tenacious professional . . . [who] can plot, coerce, compromise and charm with the best of her masculine peers" (21). But apparently that did not stop some of her party aides' worries over how they could go into the office of a woman governor "and swear at her" (21).

Rose Mofford, according to the *New York Times*, wore a "trademark . . . platinum beehive hairdo" and was "dangerous with a one-liner. She is a raucous quipster who antagonizes almost no one and disarms almost everyone with political barbs. . . . She was a star athlete, winning national honors in softball. She was also a prize-winning typist" (Gruson 26). *Newsweek* also claimed that Mofford was "not exactly the classic picture of a politician, what with a doll collection in her office and her name in the phone book . . . the improbable 'grandmother of Arizona' " (Foote 27). She was described as a "Mae West look-alike, or 'Tammy Faye in 10 years' " (27). In the Kansas gubernatorial race, *Newsweek* declared that Finney's candidacy was disorienting. She "is not only an ardent right-to-lifer but a Democrat and a woman to boot. . . . The role-reversing contest has dismayed many voters" (Salholz 34).

Newsweek claimed that Ann Richards "looks like a suburban matron, talks like a good ole boy and works a crowd like a trench-savvy politician." Despite her reputation "as an able manager . . . she seems an unlikely governor of Texas" (Pedersen 22). Molly Ivins explained: "Ann Richards is smart and tough and funny and pretty, which I notice just confuses the hell out of a lot of people." What makes men uncomfortable is "seeing a pretty woman be bitingly funny. You can tell they think it's an extremely dangerous combination" (Ivins 26). She "is living proof that appearances can be dangerously deceptive. She seems, well, like somebody's grandmother . . . [and] also a hard-nosed politician" (Plummer and Maier 85). And not to be outdone, several sources point out that Jane Hull is more likely known as the "Iron Lady" of Arizona than by her official title of governor ("Jane" 1).

What these descriptions emphasize is that even though women can be all these things, there is something unfitting, unlikely, or disorienting going on. Instead of confronting the masculine norms of political culture that work to keep women in place, the woman governor is the one who is out of bounds. Instead of acknowledging the ways that political practice works rhetorically, the rationality guiding political participation takes precedence.

These four clusters of metaphors—governor as pioneer, puppet, beauty queen, and unruly woman—provide the constructions that current women political executives must negotiate. The final cluster is pivotal and crucial to successful negotiation of the prevailing liberal democratic leadership culture by women. If recent women governors were to transform such metaphors successfully, the resultant image would not be one that attempted to fuse together two dichotomous and gendered terms, but rather one more transformative, seeing political leaders as chief executives without the necessity of a feminine qualifier or fear of appearing overly masculine or of effacing a husband's masculinity. Such stretching would give male politicians more latitude as well.

This is an issue that women such as Whitman and Kunin acknowledged. Whitman was quoted in the *Chicago Tribune*: "Where a man is considered strong, a woman is considered bitchy. Where a man is decisive, a woman is shrill. There is a double standard, but if you're spending your entire time railing against it, you won't get anything done" ("Quotes" 2). And, according to Kunin:

At some gut level, the art of politics—combative, competitive, self-asserting—is sometimes difficult to integrate with our feminine selves. . . . Each step builds a new self-image, enabling us to move from the passive to the active voice. . . . We will not accept that there is a permanent dichotomy between being in charge and being feminine. Our goal is to humanize this world by combining both; let us begin. (qtd. in "On Political" 84)

Chapter Three

Portrait of a "Governor Lady": An Examination of Nellie Tayloe Ross's Autobiographical Political Advocacy

Jennifer Burek Pierce

Following her tenure as the first woman elected governor in the United States, Nellie Tayloe Ross wrote a three-part autobiography describing her life and her experience as Wyoming's governor from 1925 to 1927 for *Good Housekeeping*. Published not long after Ross's defeat in the regular 1927 state election, the autobiography titled "The Governor Lady" incorporates moments of personal and public significance. Together, these public and private moments demonstrated to American women not only Ross's accomplishments but a potential connection between their own lives and public life. This story of a woman's entry into American politics has received scant attention from scholars, including those who focus on the history of rhetoric and public address.

Ross's virtual disappearance from public prominence is a feature of later times, rather than her own. She became a recognized political figure after winning a 1924 election to determine who would fill the remainder of her husband's gubernatorial term following his sudden death. Ross received considerable attention from her contemporaries, ranging from photographers, movie makers, and magazine writers to a tourist who "said that he and his family had driven two hundred miles out of their way to call upon the woman governor, and had no intention of leaving without seeing her" (Ross 3: 73). After serving as Wyoming's governor, Ross continued to work in politics, first in a position in the national Democratic Party and later in another national governmental position (Vexler 61). She spoke at events throughout the country both during and after her time in office and authored opinion pieces for magazines. Ross's significance to her contemporaries is one signal that her rhetoric deserves attention.

The purpose of this chapter is to examine how Ross used the autobiography to construct a public identity in a way that allowed her to continue the dialogue about how women function in the public sphere. This project requires discussion both of Ross's words and of scholarly ideas about women's texts. Primarily, this study examines the way Ross represents her preparation for and her activities while in office. Because the narrative reflects a belief in women's abilities to move beyond conventional domestic roles, it should be understood as an argument for women to take an active role in public life, particularly in politics. While several of Ross's positions on women's rights issues are in some respects conservative, her rhetoric represents a significant effort to continue the progress of women's rights. The tensions underlying her ideas are examined in the conclusion.

THE RHETORICAL SIGNIFICANCE OF AUTOBIOGRAPHY AND WOMEN'S WORDS

Critical and rhetorical analyses of women's public discourse often challenge the rationales that have been used for preserving and evaluating women's words. Particularly in the genre of autobiography, scholars cite a need to reconsider the criteria for determining both the significance and the meaning of women's accounts of their lives. Traditional standards for assessing the significance of an autobiography are directly related to the individual's own importance and how well he or she represents the era in which he or she lived (Misch 12).

In the case of women's autobiographies, these standards can be problematic. As Sidonie Smith observes, "[v]ery few women have achieved the status of 'eminent person'; and those who have done so have more commonly been labeled 'exceptional' rather than 'representative' women" (8). Consequently, works by men are seen as having defined the form, while the socialization of women, particularly at a time when the nature of their roles was changing, created conditions that made it unlikely that women would fit within accepted paradigms of the genre. The story of Ross's life as published in *Good Housekeeping* is particularly interesting in that it falls somewhere in between the informal, unpublished autobiographical writings associated with women of earlier eras and the enduring book-length works more commonly produced by their male counterparts. Ross, then, exhibited an intermediate perspective.

Ross's work holds an interesting position in light of certain contentions about the nature of public discourse prior to the 1920s. Michael McGee presents the following image of society at that time: "Except for everyday conversations, all discourse within a particular language community was produced from the same resources. Further, all discourse found its influence on the same small class of people who comprised the political nation. And it was the same small class that received the benefits of a homogenized education" ("Text" 284). McGee describes a closed community built upon tradition, whose ideals permeated its rhetorical practices. The disruption and decline of this idyllic culture spring from the action of women: "If I were telling the story, I would likely begin with the agitation that led to the passage of the Nineteenth Amendment, the women's suffrage movement" (McGee, "Text" 285). After women began to demand a voice in politics, McGee contends that the nature of public discourse changed.

Accordingly, a number of scholars have suggested that we ask different questions about women's rhetorical activities. Carole Spitzack and Kathryn Carter argue that we need to examine women's communication not as an isolated phenomenon but as part of the spectrum of human communication. They critique standards that suggest that most women's public discourse fails as effective persuasion. "So long as women's speaking is judged according to criteria that exclude women, it will be deemed inconsequential, specialized, or lacking in persuasive appeal" (406). Instead, they write, rhetorical study should reflect on "what women say, how women use the political platform [and] how women speak" (407). These are questions well suited to the evaluation of public communication like Ross's autobiographical essays.

Indeed, the autobiographies of prominent women are increasingly being regarded as a source of information about their rhetorical activities. In "Autobiographies as Rhetorical Narratives," Martha Solomon suggests that autobiography, although not traditionally examined for rhetorical merit or political impact, be viewed as a vehicle for persuasion. She states:

If the leader of a social movement writes the story of his or her life, the narrative quite naturally will serve as an inspirational model for followers and as a tool for recruiting new members. Within these works, the author not only will recount the details of a life but may also suggest the roots of his or her commitment to the cause and the value of dedicating one's life to working for the advancement of the ideal. (355)

This possibility seems particularly significant when considering the life story of a feminist or a female political figure. Women who became public figures and wanted to persuade others that what they did was acceptable and even desirable needed to make this argument on the basis of their own lives in the absence of a tradition authorizing such activity. Martha Watson echoes this idea in her recent work *Lives of Their Own: Rhetorical Dimensions in Autobiographies of Women Activists*. She suggests that women activists who write their life stories "attest to readers about the importance, value, and significance of their causes and urge the readers' appreciation of their commitment. Their autobiographies also provide evidence of the impact of their ideology on their lives" (3). As Karlyn Kohrs Campbell writes:

Efforts will be made to create an identification with the experiences of the audience and those described by the speaker. The goal of such rhetoric is . . . persuading listeners that they can act effectively in the world. . . . Given the traditional concept of womanhood, which emphasized passivity, submissiveness, and patience, persuading women that they could act was a precondition for other kinds of persuasive efforts. (*Man* 1: 13)

Barbara Biesecker has argued against characterizing passive feminine behavior as inherently negative and activism as exclusively positive. This perspective must be acknowledged, yet Campbell's assessment is a valid one in the post-suffrage years in which Ross writes.

Historically, female autobiography accomplishes two goals. First, the author advocates change by revealing her public life but also demonstrates her position in the status quo by portraying herself as having traditional, accepted values. Solomon observes that in autobiographies of nineteenth-century feminists, the subjects' lives serve "as models for how women can both retain their femininity and assert their worthiness as people" (364). Estelle Jelinek notes that women autobiographers "concentrate on their personal lives, domestic details, family difficulties, close friends, and especially people who influenced them" (Introduction 8). The writings of Elizabeth Cady Stanton demonstrate this tendency to include details that focus on family responsibilities and de-emphasize political messages. For example, Stanton "softens her political message to the predominantly female audience . . . with humorous and distracting anecdotes about her arduous travels as a lyceum lecturer, with advice to young mothers about caring for their children" (Jelinek, Introduction 9). This strategy had its uses even after the ratification of the Nineteenth Amendment because many of the same concerns about women's roles persisted.

Managing the tensions of female autonomy versus conventional expectations, as well as the conflicting demands of public and private life, has consequences in women's autobiographies. Christine Oravec describes autobiography as a "nonfictionalized . . . report of the conditions and the qualities of life, [and] also as the strategized creation of that life in the face of strict and constraining conventional expectations" (358). Other critics agree that convention dominates reader response to women's autobiographies, pushing women to account for ingrained social attitudes when creating their life stories. Thus, women often give reasons for writing or speaking that belie a willful decision to do so based on their assessment of their importance. In addition, they describe domesticity as more important than public life and consequently, construct fragmented or episodic narratives (Jelinek, Introduction 17). Jelinek argues that "the multidimensionality of women's socially conditioned roles seems to have established a pattern of diffusion and diversity when they write their autobiographies as well" (Introduction 17). Stresses placed upon women, then, have resulted in stresses upon both the content and the form of their life stories. Although these generalizations are based largely on readings of nineteenth-century autobiography, traces of these patterns are recognizable in Ross's early twentieth-century narrative.

Her "argument from personal history" (Solomon 356) enables us to understand her words in a rich cultural context, offering ideas about daily life as well as the historical and cultural situation. Thus, the autobiography is well suited to the critical task of considering "what constituted a feminist act for a woman given her own time and cultural roots" rather than evaluating "these early women by modern theories of feminism" and our contemporary standards for women leaders (Carlson 86). If an objective of scholarship about women leaders is to "widen our definition" of feminism to "include women who may outwardly adhere to the social order, but whose rhetoric serves non-traditional ends" (Carlson 86), Ross's autobiography is a significant document in the history of women's entry into American politics.

It is worth noting that the 1920s, when Ross became governor, were times of conflicting and often contradictory public attitudes. Although the era ushered in flappers, more liberal social behavior, and the passage of the Nineteenth Amendment, this same period still espoused conventional ideas about women, which were at odds with the apparent freedom and change signaled by these phenomena. The decade that began with the appearance of new roles for women in the public sphere closed with limited progress toward this end.

Women had won suffrage and could participate in politics, yet the actuality of their situation was somewhat different from the printed words authorizing their entry into the public sphere. Campbell noted that women were not encouraged to exercise their recently gained rights (*Man* 1: 6). Likewise, Joan Hoff found that suffrage guaranteed women the right to vote but did not give them the means to enter public dialogue. In the years between the passage of the Nineteenth Amendment and World War II, few women had "true economic independence, equal social expectations, political experience, or even the educational and professional training necessary for obtaining leadership in politics" (Hoff 208). Nor was it likely that women would pursue our modern concepts of equality at this time. Some women "realized that the vote had not eliminated sex discrimination in American life, nor had protective legislation eliminated discrimination in the workplace"; however, these ideas were considered the positions of "militant suffragists" and "radical women" rather than commonly held views (Hoff 201). Under such circumstances, it should not be surprising that the initial struggle to improve women's status is generally considered to have ended by 1929.

REPRESENTATION OF ROSS AS THE "GOVERNOR LADY"

It is in this context that Nellie Tayloe Ross campaigned for and won her deceased husband's position as governor of Wyoming. Elected in 1925, Ross became the first woman in the United States to become the head of a state, and as such, she faced numerous challenges. These included the problem of constructing a public identity encompassing her role as widow, single mother, and "governor lady," as the press referred to her, while the entire country paid rapt attention to the novelty of a female governor. Her three-part autobiography, published in *Good Housekeeping* in 1927, reveals Ross's attempt to present herself as a woman with political power at a time when this was not the norm.

A recurring theme of the autobiography was the uniqueness of Ross's position. In the articles published by *Good Housekeeping*, Ross wrote that the idea that a woman should run for office was, to her knowledge and to those around her, unprecedented. Even in Wyoming, which had given women the right to vote thirty-six years before, Ross's candidacy was considered unusual. Her brother told her that the idea that she should compete for her deceased husband's office was "a remarkable suggestion" (Ross 1: 37). Others disapproved, Ross recalls: "Some of the wisest political prophets shook their heads. A woman for governor!" (Ross 1: 37). Thus, in addition to the disadvantage of being the Democratic candidate when Republicans were winning elections throughout the nation, Ross carried the stigma of being, as she put it, "an experiment [whose] every act or omission was under constant scrutiny" (2: 172).

Aware of these attitudes and "feeling that more sustained and diligent attention would be expected of [her] than would have been expected of a man" (Ross 1: 82), Ross attempted to de-emphasize her gender. For instance, she called the request of a movie maker for "a picture of the woman candidate making bread . . . or engaged in some other domestic activity" irrelevant to her role as a public figure and refused him (2: 206). In the autobiography, Ross limited discussion of her family and her role as wife and mother; references to this aspect of her life were carefully contextualized for rhetorical effect.

Public attitudes toward women created rhetorical situations that Ross had to address. Primarily, she needed to establish a strong ethos. In the autobiography, she detailed how she accomplished this task by recounting incidents that demonstrate integrity, independence, loyalty, and frugality.

Initially reluctant to become a candidate for the governorship, Ross was convinced to compete for office when another politician told her that the legislature might be willing to provide a governor's widow with a stipend. She found this proposition unethical, writing that "he crystallized my determination to take no money from the state . . . unless I gave in return a service commensurate with the award" (1: 206). When campaigning for re-election, Ross told a reporter that "she was carrying on a campaign on the highest moral plane" and that "she had a high personal regard for those who were opposing her candidacy" (qtd. in Hendricks 91). Ross asserted that politicians' motto should be "If we do not always meet with success at the hands of the people, at least we should strive to deserve it" (91). Ross wanted her audience to believe that she sought office because of her commitment to her husband and his ideals, as well as her ethical principles. She wrote that others requested she become a candidate for office on the basis of her knowledge of William Bradford Ross's plans for governing the state (Ross 1: 206).

Once elected, she established the objective of monitoring the state's budget to make certain officials did not waste funds by overspending or paying appointees for inadequate work performances (Ross 2: 213). She also fought state legislators' efforts to remove her control over the appointment of bank examiners. She told them in conference that she was the best representative of "the despairing people who had lost all their savings through the failure of banks" and counted on "a disinterested authority to stand between the bankers and the depositors" (2: 215). By working to ensure the appropriate use of state money, Ross told her audience she accomplished two things: First, she upheld her husband's ideals, and secondly, she kept her own promise to prove the abilities of women in positions of public trust. Ross, then, used these passages of her autobiography to illustrate her compliance with conventional expectations of officeholders but in doing so made an argument for the idea of the competence and abilities of women politicians.

The issue of a woman's competency has a significant place in this autobi-ography. Like Ross's efforts to establish her ethos by describing her charac-ter and frugality, her recollections of her preparations for and her actions in office can be seen as having a two-fold aim. In addition to demonstrating her own fitness for office, by constructing a relationship between women's or-dinary activities and what she has done, Ross described the preparation of women for paid public work.

Ross portrayed herself as an intellectual partner to her husband and the successor to his political goals. In addition, she created a glimpse into their relationship, depicting it as informed by equality. First, she described her husband, William Bradford Ross, as a man devoted to his family. Conse-quently, "he almost invariably rose when the children called at night, though they nearly always called for their mother" (Ross 1: 118). Ross's depiction of her husband's interest in his family demonstrated his willingness to as-sume some domestic responsibilities.

At the same time, though, Ross took on some of her husband's profes-sional duties; these included speech writing, sometimes under deadline pres-sure. She referred briefly to events surrounding President Warren G. Harding's death, when she and her husband "sat up til dawn, preparing the ad-dress that [William Ross] was to deliver the next day at the memorial cere-mony at Sheridan" (Ross 1: 124). Another time, "when the pressure was especially strong, he came hurrying down the Mansion and asked me to help him prepare a Labor Day proclamation. Time was short . . . so putting our heads together, we evolved one that expressed what he wanted to say" (1: 124). These incidents, related briefly, indicate a degree of interchangeability of traditional gender roles in the Ross household.

The intellectual pursuits of Ross and her husband constituted her pri-mary preparation for office. Ross and other women of her generation were not educated in the same way that their husbands and other men were. Training to become politicians and public speakers, then, must have oc-curred outside the formal education of women such as Ross. A contempo-rary biographical article refers briefly to her possessing a "liberal mental background, gained through travel and education in private schools" before mentioning the contribution of "years of close association with her hus-band" to Ross's "intimate and accurate knowledge of state affairs" (Donaldson 9). This informal education acquired from her husband and others is described in greater detail in the autobiography.

Ross explained that much of the learning she considered valuable to her work as governor was provided by reading and discussing subjects with her husband and by participating in an intellectual women's club. She wrote:

At the beginning of our married life, every new case was a real event to the almost briefless young lawyer and his wife. . . . When he wanted to test the effect of his theories of the law by discussion with me, he could depend on finding a ready listener and one not unwilling to expose any fallacies I thought I could detect. . . . I did not then realize I was absorbing an understanding of law and government that was to prove invaluable to me in later years. (Ross 1: 124)

When her husband became governor, Ross continued to assist with his responsibilities. She recounted having discussed his "problems and plans" for the state and helping him write speeches under deadline pressure (Ross 1: 124). In effect, Ross told her readers that her husband was like a mentor to her and that her assistance to him served her interests as well as his.

In addition to her husband's professional matters, the couple's entertainment, which included reading "classics of proved worth" (1: 118), contributed to Ross's abilities to meet the demands of public speaking once elected to state office. Ross recommended "to young married people this practice of reading aloud, not only as a source of pleasure, but as a means of supplemental education" (1: 118). She valued the subject matter of the books but found the activity had merit, too: "even the strengthening of my voice by the exercise of reading aloud would prove, upon the public platform, an asset beyond price!" (1: 118). Her praise of the Cheyenne Woman's Club, another of her leisure activities, described the intellectual opportunities she and other women found in such organizations. As she noted:

Hundreds of women the country over have developed in women's clubs talents worthy of national renown, which . . . constitute an invaluable contribution toward the elevation of our intellectual standards. To the Cheyenne Woman's Club I am indebted for the development of qualities that helped me meet the demands of public office. It was something like the training men receive in county boards, municipal councils, and legislative halls. It is an experience that sharpens the wits and develops the gift of expression, particularly oral expression. (1: 119)

Thus, Ross was trained in public speaking and in political practices that were not part of the traditional contemporary curriculum of women's education.

Ross noted that she gained experience, which she would not have had otherwise because of her sex, but importantly, it should be apparent that other women also have access to similar opportunities. Her interest in her husband's career was that of "the usual loyal wife," and "hundreds of women" belonged to clubs like the one in which she participated (Ross 1: 31, 119). While these domestic and feminine activities are not the stuff of which present-day feminists are made, Ross credited them with a significant contribution to her ability to take on professional responsibilities normally reserved for men.

Experience in the domestic sphere, Ross told her audience, enhances women's competence. She recounted the struggle of caring for sick children and connected it to her political responsibilities. "It may well be asked what sort of training was this for future official service to Wyoming. Simply this: the demands of the day, which could not be ignored, evaded, or postponed, challenged and strengthened every resource of which I was possessed" (Ross 1: 118). This is one instance in which Ross revealed the details of her domestic life for persuasive purposes. Like the nineteenth-century feminists before her who were "careful to portray themselves as ordinary women" (Solomon 364), Ross informed her readers that she faced concerns and worries like their own. One message of the autobiography is that her life is far from unusual, that domestic arts and other activities, which have traditionally been part of a woman's life, may be used to produce something besides a well-run household.

Some critics have noted a dissonance in women's autobiographies, claiming that the personal details do not mesh with the articulation of the public role (Jelinek, *Tradition* 385; Solomon 355). In "The Governor Lady," Ross's movement between public and private spheres does not strain the unity of her story. Strategic and skillful use of the materials of her life as wife and mother along with the occurrences of her work as politician and governor makes the two appear compatible. The divergent elements of her life are brought together in her role as governor of Wyoming.

It should be acknowledged, however, that the image of Ross as a neutral, competent figure whose sex was not a factor in her public dealings may be more a creation of her autobiography than a perception shared by those who interacted with her. While her biographers agreed that Ross was intelligent and able to deal with the demands of public office, their remarks clearly indicated that Ross's femininity was very much on the public's mind. Indeed, one contemporary writer commented that while Ross wanted her "administration to be judged upon its merits" (Ross qtd. in Donaldson 7), it was "a bit difficult to think of Governor Ross as simply a 'genderless executive' " (Donaldson 7). The reader's attention is called to Ross's "cameo-like features" of "the essentially feminine type" (7). In addition, Lee Donaldson attributed Ross's political success to the following habits: "She courts advice (always a flattering characteristic). . . . She writes a charming note in return for a little favor. She remembers to send flowers. She remembers names and faces" (8). Another reporter who observed Ross on the campaign trail noted that the band that heralded her entrance to the speaking platform routinely did so by playing "Let Me Call You Sweetheart" (Hendricks 84). Thus, whereas Ross made efforts to tell readers how she exercised abilities that could be used regardless of one's sex, other observers noted both her skills *and* her femininity.

There is an explanation for this discrepancy when the autobiography is considered as a persuasive message directed toward women as citizens and potential professionals. Ross's description of her preparation for and her actions in office had a two-fold aim. In addition to demonstrating her own strengths and fitness for office, by constructing a relationship between women's ordinary activities and what she has done, Ross effectively made a case for many women's abilities to take on paid professional work. Accentuating her personal qualities as reporters did would interfere with this implicit argument.

Nonetheless, discussion of the importance of her accomplishment also involved Ross's use of features of women's life experiences to function in the public sphere. While assuring female readers of her and their own competence at managing more than their families and kitchens, Ross noted that she was frequently asked whether women truly belonged in public office. Her answer, which concluded her autobiography, affirmed women's competency: "I can see no reason why women, who have so unmistakably demonstrated their ability to fill with credit places of responsibility in every other field they have invaded, may not aspire to take a place at the head of any branch of this government" (3: 131).

While Ross believed experience proves women capable of leadership, she still held the "personal conviction" that "it is in the realm of the home . . . that woman fulfills her highest destiny and finds her greatest happiness" (Ross 1:118). She explained her own entry into politics with words that echo the deflective strategies often found in nineteenth-century women's autobiographies: "Divine intervention changed the circumstances of my life, leaving me in a position to assume public responsibilities" (Ross 3: 131). This statement, more than any other aspect of the narrative, seems to respond to contemporary conventions and audience expectations.

Ross contended that a woman who chose to focus on domestic responsibilities must, however, remain intellectually and politically active. Citing the need for ethical practices in government to ensure a good environment for families and a strong country, Ross insisted that women work to shape politics for the better through party affiliation and informed voting. She argued that:

Women must . . . speak a new language in politics, which in effect is this—that never, through their votes knowingly and deliberately given, shall the country be delivered into the hands of unscrupulous public officials. Thus they may serve notice that the political party which descends to practises [*sic*] inconsistent with high ideals of Americanism, does so at the deadly peril of losing the whole woman vote. (3:197)

Having shown that the ordinary events of women's lives prepare them for other responsibilities, Ross advocated that women become politically active even if they did not become officeholders.

CONCLUSION

One question that might arise from critical assessment of Ross's autobiography, particularly its end, is why she did not more emphatically or directly endorse women's entry into leadership roles in the public sphere. In other words, how can a woman who proclaimed the importance of family over a profession be recognized as a true leader of women's political activism? Two things must be considered when assessing the impact of Ross's political career on women's roles. First, contemporary goals of feminist activity differ significantly from those of Ross's era. And second, if Ross's public had not perceived that she accepted the cultural values of her time, she would not have gained the public voice that she had.

Both Biesecker and Oravec call attention to societal constraints that make voicing certain ideas implausible, and the contemporary position of women and attitudes toward feminism in the 1920s suggest an explanation for Ross's articulated preference for women's role in the domestic sphere. Despite having gained the right to vote and having achieved business and professional positions in increasing numbers (Stricker 479), women did not have equality or a strong public presence. Their entry into public and political realms was still somewhat novel.

Furthermore, the perception of the woman's rights movement as extremist would decrease the chance of the success of an openly feminist agenda, and Ross's experience with partisan politics in Wyoming government made her more aware of the importance of accomplishing goals with minimal conflict. Her invocations of women's responsibilities to their families and the moral influence that they possess were not simply conventional adages about women's place in society, as these views have come to be regarded. Instead, they allowed her to speak from a position that most of her audience could identify and accept.

Also, while Ross wrote that women are happiest at home, it should be observed that the details she gave about her own domestic experience suggest that it was atypical or unconventional in some respects. Even before her husband's death, Ross's life had strong intellectual and political elements.

Furthermore, in the concluding paragraphs of her autobiography, she told her audience that to truly provide good homes, they must make their voices heard in the political process. In doing so, Ross enlarged the scope of the domestic sphere. This autobiographical narrative makes the case that being a wife and mother involved intellectual pursuits and involvement with the public sphere.

What we can understand, then, about the conflict between Ross's political role and her conventional concluding message is that regardless of whatever beliefs she had about the abilities of women, she faced cultural restrictions on articulating a message that we would regard as truly endorsing women's leadership capabilities. As Cheree Carlson reminds us, " 'Feminism' is often perceived negatively by women and men in our culture. It clearly threatens traditional white middle class notions that are still largely accept[able]" to the general public (96). In the face of cultural constraints, Ross articulated her gubernatorial experience as a successful one, as evidence for her claim that "women . . . may . . . aspire to take a place at the head of any branch of government" (Ross 3: 131). She achieved an unusual position and used it to urge women to reconsider the nature of their roles.

Ross's autobiography for readers of *Good Housekeeping* created an intricate image. Using the resources and the values of her audience, she argued for change, and she did so in a way that embellished, rather than rent, the social fabric. As such, "The Governor Lady" not only explained what Ross accomplished in politics but also invited other women to participate in public life in whatever way was best suited to their individual experiences.

Chapter Four

"For Kentucky": The Shared Vision of Governor Martha Layne Collins

Alma Hall

As governor of Kentucky from 1984 to 1988, Martha Layne Collins saw the everyday in a new way. Artistlike, she painted a change for Kentucky that inextricably combined economic development and improvements in education. Prior administrations had focused on one at the expense of the other, but Collins understood that the future she wanted for Kentucky demanded an educated workforce and opportunities for their employment at a level above minimum wage. The decade since has sustained her prediction.

Early in her administration, Collins laid the groundwork for a national model of education reform and brought Toyota Manufacturing of North America to Georgetown, Kentucky. While she receives less credit for her role in education reform because it was not funded and implemented for several years, these events fulfilled a desire she had shared with legislators during the opening session of the Kentucky legislature in January 1984. This chapter questions how Collins achieved such profound change in a state known to elect few women to statewide office and at a time when women were largely excluded from top positions in any organization. Examining Collins' speeches to the Kentucky legislature and her reports of meetings with manufacturers, this study suggests that Collins' ability to look at issues and events through multiple cognitive perspectives persuaded by providing what Gronbeck refers to as a "framework of shared meaning" with the legislators and with foreign manufacturers (13).

Collins' ability to reframe governmental issues and events congnitively has been previously documented and correlated to her effectiveness as a leader (Hall). In that study, I examined a group of nationally prominent women to explore the ways in which some women lead effectively despite powerful, socially shared images to the contrary. The findings of that study supported Lee Bolman and Terrence Deal's research that primarily measured men in top leadership positions. They reported a correlation between leadership effectiveness and the use of multiple frames, particularly the symbolic and political frames, to understand organizational issues and events. While Bolman and Deal link the use of multiple frames to leadership effectiveness, they do not examine specifically how a leader creates change through communication. They do assert that the use of the symbolic frame creates meaning from ambiguity and that the communication of a strong vision creates loyalty among followers. They do acknowledge, when discussing the origin of a vision, that "leadership is a two-way street" (315). Yet, with the following anecdote, they illustrate that managers need to find new ways to see things and must "articulate and communicate their vision so others can also learn to shift perspectives" (12): A critic once commented to Cézanne, "That [painting] doesn't look anything like a sunset." Pondering his painting, Cézanne responded, "Then you don't see sunsets the way I do" (Bolman and Deal 12).

These leadership theorists assert that meaning is the most basic of human needs and that leaders who use the symbolic frame make ambiguous events meaningful. They also seem to be saying, at least as noted above, that conception and articulation of an event come totally from the leader. Therefore, framing includes both the act of defining an event and the assertion of that definition. Such a notion harkens back to an abandoned understanding of rhetoric in which the target receives a message designed to persuade (Gronbeck 13).

In my initial study of Collins (Hall), I documented perceived leadership effectiveness and correlated it to the use of multiple frames, but I did not specifically examine how leader communication created organizational change. Neither Bolman and Deal nor I have examined cognitive framing and re-framing as a rhetorical process. Questions remain about the relationship between leadership effectiveness and framing and cognitive complexity. Does the leader frame and re-frame an issue in a way that illuminates that definition for others? Does change come about when leader and follower mutually persuade by developing shared meaning?

Neither communication nor leadership scholars have addressed this total relationship to a great extent. Most leadership theorists look at one or two of the aspects in isolation. J. Thomas Wren provides the exception. By definition he links re-framing, the ability to view a problem from multiple perspectives, to cognitive complexity. He calls re-framing one of the essential elements of critical thinking and, thus, a necessary leadership competency (375). He does not, however, examine how cognitive framing creates change.

Communication scholars who have attempted to bridge the relationship gap similarly look at one or two aspects in isolation. For example, cognitive complexity has long been included as a measure of communication competence, but the link between cognitive complexity and leadership effectiveness has been much more tenuous (Barge 181). Karl Kuhnert and Philip Lewis are among the few hinting at the notion that cognitive complexity is a necessary ingredient for effective leadership. They do so by applying Robert Kegan's integrated theories of constructivism and development to gain a better understanding of leadership effectiveness. Kegan argues that cognitive-developmental theory is more than a theory of cognition; it is a theory about emotion as well. He goes on to outline five levels of subject-object relations that depict a helix of lifetime growth through which individuals move back and forth, integrating and differentiating in each stage. Of greater importance to the discussion of cognitive complexity and leadership, Kegan purports that institutional emotional life, or stage four, is "a matter of holding both sides of a feeling simultaneously" whereas interpersonal life, stage three, "tends to experience its ambivalences one side at a time" (101). Kuhnert and Lewis juxtapose Kegan's stages of development with the concept of transactional leadership. They contend that a leader must be able to operate at Kegan's higher, stage-four institutional level in order to transform followers. They reason that only an individual who has attained an identity that has reincorporated the interpersonal level into the institutional level (that is, those who "have relationships" rather than those who "are relationships") will be able to go beyond the interpersonal needs and conflicts of others to pursue their own end values.

Theodore Zorn's theories echo those of Kuhnert and Lewis. However, Zorn goes somewhat further in integrating cognitive complexity and communication competence and leadership theory by linking effectiveness to the leader's level of cognitive complexity. In a study that called for both the leader and the follower to recall a message that had occurred some weeks prior, Zorn reported a moderate association between construct system development and transformational leadership.

Patricia Witherspoon provides the most concrete link between framing and persuasion, but she does not integrate cognitive complexity into the relationship. Like Bolman and Deal, Witherspoon regards leaders as managers of meaning, but she is more specific. "When initiating change they [leaders] must use the rhetorical concept of 'identification' to bridge differences between them and organizational members" (*Communicating* 136). She asserts that framing, fundamentally a communication process, provides the context that gives meaning to a message and that leaders use communication strategies to create change by changing the perspectives of organizational members (*Communicating* 136–139).

In addition to questions about the relationship between leadership effectiveness and framing and cognitive complexity, this inquiry must examine the image of leader as male, since in popular perceptions men are viewed as more cognitively complex than women. My earlier research reported no difference between the cognitive frames used by effective male or female leaders, but it did acknowledge the tremendous bias against women attaining top positions in organizations. For example, I reported that while women's entry into the workforce has been called the single most important change to occur in the American labor market in the last half century, their positions in organizations have changed only slightly since Title VII of the Civil Rights Act of 1964 prohibited sexual discrimination in employment (Hall 4).

Various scholars have provided explanations for this phenomenon, but most considered women lacking in some way that made them unsuited to leadership. Rosabeth. Moss Kanter suggested that women do not have access to power in the positions they fill, while Betty Harragan believed women lacked the team and military experience necessary to play the corporate game and win. *In Breaking the Glass Ceiling: Can Women Reach the Top of America's Largest Corporations*, Ann Morrison, Randall White, and Ellen Van Velsor argue that women have not found a way through the glass ceiling. Authors Eliza Collins, Agnes Missirian, and Belle Ragins independently found that women lack mentors. According to Levinson, women lacked career dreams that incorporated all their relationships in their lives (see Johnson 41–43), while Barbara Bools and Lydia Swan found that women's values often did not align with those of many organizations. Nissim Aranya, Talma Kushnir, and Aharon Valency contend that, as a rule, women do not have sufficient job commitment: Hazel Ezell, Charles Odewahn, and J. Daniel Sherman suggest they lack high expectations, motivation, and confidence. In *Finding Herself: Pathways to Identity Development in Women*, Ruthellen Josselson concludes that women typically do not have the ability to translate personal relationships into global concerns. Finally, Maccoby and Thorne and Luria argue that women's interpersonal communication skills do not effectively influence men.

Even a cursory analysis of these *perceived* inadequacies suggests that views of leadership effectiveness are based on male images of leadership. Kentucky offered no exception to the male image of leader in the early 1980s. Even today, according to Linda Blackford's editorial reprinted in the *Lexington Herald-Leader* and a feature article researched by Angie Muhs, women haven't yet found their place in state politics in Kentucky. In the

United States, an average of 21.8 percent of state legislators are women; the percentage of women serving in the Kentucky legislature stands at just 9.4 percent, ahead only of Alabama. In addition, since Collins only one woman, Peppy Martin, the unsuccessful Republican Candidate in 1999, has made a serious run for the office of governor.

How did Collins, a woman, persuade an automobile manufacturing company, a segment of the manufacturing economy that has been traditionally biased against women, from a male-dominated culture such as Japan to locate their U.S. plant in Kentucky? How did she persuade the state legislature to appropriate money for that relocation? Answers to these questions are best discovered in the natural interaction between leader and follower. Governor Collins' speeches, supplied publicly by Kentucky Educational Television, provide a record of such natural interaction. Televised news coverage by all of the stations in Frankfort, the state capital, and the major cities of Louisville and Lexington of the four years she served as governor extends this analysis, as does Governor Collins' recollections of some events. In a typical ethnographic tradition, data are analyzed as presented. Analysis is grounded in the theoretical perspectives of leadership presented by Bolman and Deal, who divide organizational theory into four distinct frames—structural, human resource, political, and symbolic. The study then examines the intersection of cognitive framing and rhetorical effectiveness.

Bolman and Deal hypothesize that individuals generally prefer to utilize one or perhaps two of the frames to organize, gather, and explain organizational phenomena. Most individuals employ either the structural frame, which emphasizes roles and the setting of clear directions and solving problems by restructuring, or they utilize the human resource frame to view organizational problems in terms of individual needs. Both perspectives account more for effective management than effective leadership, which requires use of the political and symbolic frames.

Leaders who operate within the political frame assume that competition for resources is a given and build coalitions to succeed. Those who view organizational phenomena through the symbolic frame inspire loyalty by communicating a strong vision. The symbolic frame, based primarily in the theoretical discipline of anthropology, asserts that meaning is the most basic of human needs and, thus, depends heavily on communication. Leaders who utilize the symbolic frame recognize that events are often ambiguous. They create or translate stories of personal vision, stories that tell of wanting things to be better, not for them but for society, a wanting that translates into a sense of purpose.

When Governor Collins opened her "State of the Commonwealth Address" by acknowledging that "no other governing body since the Depression has had so little money to work with," she immediately re-framed that limitation into a symbolic opportunity: "You and I working over the next few months . . . will make things better for our people. . . . We owe it to our people." She thereby symbolically re-framed the issue of money, "Tight money is no excuse for a poverty of ideas." By doing so, Collins set up an expectation that the legislators, too, must re-frame their views.

Typical of those who view events and issues through the symbolic frame, Collins recognizes that individuals have a need to make sense of events in their lives. She resolves ambiguity by creating a vision that reflects her wanting things better not just for herself but for those she represents—"for Kentucky." What at first might seem to be a human resource perspective, as she tells of meeting Kentuckians one-to-one, more accurately reflects the symbolic use of stories. What at first might seem to be a view through the structural frame, as she discusses differing roles and responsibilities, more likely evidences her symbolic understanding of what it is to be a leader. She incorporates the political frame to share her perspective with the legislators:

We know each other. We're friends. We've worked together in the past and we will work together now to lead Kentucky through these hard times, toward a brighter to-morrow. We'll manage this government fairly but with a tight fist. But that's not enough. Management can only carry us so far. Managers marshal resources; lead-ers provide direction. We must always remember that government is more than a business. [She then received the first applause of the speech because the preceding governor, John Y. Brown, one of the founders of Kentucky Fried Chicken, had cre-ated a slogan "Oh Kentucky!" that encompassed the need to run the state like a busi-ness.] Government exists to serve the people. Let us never forget that. ("State")

Collins specifically developed her desire for the better-educated, better-employed Kentuckian as she traveled the state during her campaign and immediately after she was elected. Using the political frame, she shares that desire and creates alliances with legislators as she identifies with the needs of their districts.

I know the people of Kentucky. You know the people of your district. I have seen your respect for them. I have seen your affection for them here in Frankfort. I've walked the main street of Whitesburg with the representative from Letcher and stopped at the drug store across from the court house and heard coal miners talk about not being able to find work. The senator from Davies and I talked with busi-nessmen in Owensboro who wondered if they could hold out until the economy im-proved. In Bowling Green, with the senator and representative, I talked with faculty and students in the Faculty House on the campus of Western Kentucky University about their hopes for education. In Breckenridge the senator and I talked with farm-

ers worried about holding on to their family farms. The representative from Campbell and I visited with senior citizens one morning and I remember them telling me
how much trouble they were having buying food after they paid for their housing
and medicine. I talked to people on the streets of Louisville. Unemployed factory
workers wanted to see new industry. The representative from Greenup and I met in
a union hall in Ashland. Labor must be involved in the change of Kentucky. In
Fulton the representative and I talked with parents who wondered if their children
were getting an education that would provide them with a satisfying, well-paying
job. What I'm saying is that I know the hopes and dreams of your people. ("State")

In the next segment of the 1984 "State of the Commonwealth Address,"
Collins restates her responsibility as a leader. Furthermore, she expresses
herself as a leader symbolically as an extension of her identity rather than as
the performance of a position, which would have indicated a use of the
structural frame. In other words, Collins rhetorically frames her notion that
leaders create and regulate change for the good of the whole. She acknowledges that legislators provide service to a more selected audience. By en-
casing the concept of roles within these cultural identities, Collins builds
what Witherspoon refers to as identification and Gronbeck calls "the frameworks of shared meanings" (13). Collins says:

I know the responsibility you feel toward your people. In a sense you each bring
here tonight a special part of Kentucky. . . . Your people expect much of you. Over
the years this legislature has evolved into a full partner in governing Kentucky and I
respect that independence [*applause*]. I will work with you. I will always listen to
you, but I count on you to represent your district. I ask you to understand that my responsibility is much broader. My responsibility is to all Kentucky so, as I respect
your independence and closeness to the people of your district, I ask that you respect my broader obligation. ("State")

Collins offers another framework for shared meaning when she calls for
the legislature to embark on what Gronbeck refers to as a collective journey:
"I have been elected governor in a time of change that is transforming our
lives. If we are to avoid being left behind in these times, we must improve
our schools. . . . I have never seen such wide consensus. Kentuckians want
better schools" ("State"). She also politically re-frames the issue of education reform by acknowledging the varied groups throughout the state who
were working to better education. In what has become her trademark, Collins says, "I intend to pull all these groups together" ("State").

Relying again on the symbolic frame to explain ambiguous events, Collins clarifies the lack of state funds: (1) from 1979 to 1983, during the economic recession, unemployment in the state doubled; (2) past state budgets

used non-recurring funds to meet annual needs; and (3) the federal government shifted to states such costs as Medicaid ("State"). In speaking of the lack of money, she re-frames the issue optimistically and calls for judicious use of the money that is available. She offers the opportunity to share meaning by reminding the legislators that they were not elected to "just get by." She calls for change in spite of limited funding. Most significantly, Collins re-frames for the legislators the issues of education and jobs. While she encourages a focus on education as the number one priority, she prophetically states: "The issue of jobs and education cannot be separated"("State").

As noted earlier, prior governors of Kentucky had tended to be either for education or for economic development. Collins profoundly tied the two—and they remain so today. She looked into a future where, without educational improvement and better jobs, Kentucky would remain in what she termed the economic backwater as the world moved into the information age. She elevated labor to a cabinet status and insisted that labor must be involved in educational improvements. These changes clearly reflected a symbolic move rather than a structural redesign.

In her 1984 "State of the Commonwealth Address" Collins utilized the political and symbolic frames to identify with the legislators. She also used those perspectives to make sense of ambiguous events and then re-framed the problems facing Kentuckians so that solutions would be found. She exhibited what has become her trademark political skill, pulling together the coalitions needed to effect change. Most of all, she evidenced a clear understanding of herself as a leader who operates at Kegan's stage-four, institutional level and transforms followers. She does so by taking a "collective journey" and creating "frameworks of shared meaning."

Collins' second major address to the public, delivered on March 15, 1984, differed drastically in style and effectiveness. Early in the legislative session, she had recognized that her proposed state budget required additional revenue. So she directed her efforts to the public through an address carried over Kentucky Educational Television. She said:

I recognize that it is not politically expedient to ask for a tax increase. When I took the oath of office I took on the responsibility to do what is right and best for the people of Kentucky. I take that responsibility more seriously than anything I have ever done in my life. I wrestled with the decision [to ask for tax increases to pay for education reform]. I considered and reconsidered every possibility. I prayed about it and in the end I knew that my obligation as Governor required that I call for the reforms I have asked for in revenues and in education. ("Major Policy")

The requested budget increases, however, were not funded by the legislature at that time. Explanations for the failure of Collins' tax package include the obvious: Tax increases are never popular. The request followed too closely her campaign promise not to raise taxes. Both explanations were likely true. They may not fully explain the lack of her success, however. While Collins talked of her understanding of the role of leader, she spoke of that role more in terms of the structural frame. She referred to an upbringing that had socialized her to not "just get by." She suggested that the legislature had not been elected to "just get by" either, but her style of speaking, specifically the frequent use of "I," offered much less of an opportunity for the legislature to develop a shared meaning. Rather, her statements appeared to target both the public and the legislature with the need for change. While she expressed that need passionately and clearly, she bore full responsibility. She failed to allow for a shared vision, for shared meaning. And, she failed to persuade.

Slightly more than a year later, in an address to a special session of the legislature on July 8, 1985, Collins symbolically framed for the legislators that "extraordinary sessions are for extraordinary events" ("Address") as she requested support for education reform. Citing the personal example of an IBM worker who had been retrained four times, Collins tied education to the ability of Kentuckians to adapt to the rapidly changing world in which they lived. She again stressed, through the political frame, that she represented all Kentuckians, from Flatwood to Dixon to Covington to Tompkinsville. Symbolically, she included mention of five previous governors, one a Republican, in the historic occasion.

While this speech did not gain immediate financial support for education reform from the state legislators, it was a rhetorical success because it framed the need for change. Massive education reform eventually required a Kentucky Supreme Court decision to uphold it, but the new governor and legislators immediately embraced the court's decision. That process of legislative change began during the Collins administration.

Not all of Governor Collins' rhetorical successes occurred before the legislative body, but these additional examples of discourse nonetheless evidence similar cognitive re-framing and her reliance on the symbolic and political frames. In telling the story of Toyota's selection of Kentucky for their manufacturing plant, Collins recalled that she had been notified that the Japanese site team would visit Tennessee first and then come to Kentucky. This Japanese site visit team had narrowed their choices to Tennessee and Kentucky. Collins acknowledged that she had felt pressure because the public perceived that she had allowed Tennessee to gain the General Motors Saturn plant some months previously. In fact, Collins said that she had chosen not to offer General Motors the incentives they wanted because they were moving workers in from factories that were cutting back or closing. She wanted additional jobs for her Kentuckians.

As recounted in a personal interview, Collins planned an early dinner at the governor's mansion, a decision strictly adhering to what she knew was the desire of the Japanese delegation to be finished by about 9:00 PM. Her behavior at this point typified the use of the symbolic frame. She knew that the Japanese loved the Stephen Foster songs, so she invited the cast of the Stephen Foster Story, in costume, to serve as the evening's entertainment. She knew the Japanese loved fireworks, so she planned eclairs with sparklers for dessert, followed by fireworks to be shot off over the state capitol building, which was next door. She personally waited to greet them at the Lexington airport. She waited and she waited.

In what she later learned may have been Tennessee's downfall, their representatives had taken the Japanese delegation to visit a site and then, upon learning from them that the site was not suitable, they had continued their bus trip to another location. Visiting this additional site then made the Japanese late for their visit with Kentucky and kept Collins waiting at the airport for approximately two hours. The Japanese arrived tired and humiliated.

Ever gracious and concerned about the welfare of others, Collins made sure that the Japanese delegation was bused directly to their hotel and that for their benefit they had already been checked in when they disembarked the bus. They were presented with welcoming gifts and allowed to freshen up. They were then taken to the party. And party they did. Collins can still recall that they clapped their hands and tapped their toes to the Stephen Foster songs. They also sang along. And, they knew all of the words to "My Old Kentucky Home"; they did not just join in at the refrain "weep no more my lady," as most of the natives do on Derby Day! The Japanese announced Georgetown, Kentucky, as their selected site the very next week.

Despite the overwhelming image of leaders as male throughout history and especially in her own state, Martha Layne Collins effected phenomenal and lasting change in Kentucky when she served as governor. The measure of that effectiveness does not rest on my earlier study ratings alone. Collins is held in esteem by state historian James H. Klotter, who, when asked to list the ten most important things that Kentuckians had done for themselves in this century, included their willingness to elect Martha Layne Collins as governor. Also, Collins was acclaimed one of the "baker's dozen of Kentuckians who have been most influential during this century" (A. Smith F1). That list of thirteen Kentuckians included authors Robert Penn Warren, Harriett Simpson Arnow, and Thomas Merton—even boxer Muhammed Ali—but the list included no other governors.

The impact of Collins' leadership can be supported as well by a factual comparison of Kentuckians' personal income by industry that was reported by the Bureau of Economic Analysis (Crouch). Long sustained by coal mining and tobacco farming, Kentuckians today would suffer real economic hardship without the increase they have experienced in manufacturing jobs. Income from coal mining has dropped about 30 percent from 1980 to 1996. Although farm earnings more than doubled during this period, income from tobacco farming has become precarious now that tobacco companies have settled government lawsuits.

Personal income from manufacturing more than doubled during the comparison period, and all of Kentucky reaped the benefits. Toyota's practice of "just in time" receipt of parts meant that all but 2 of the 120 counties, not just the "golden triangle" of Lexington, Louisville, and northern Kentucky, participated in the economic renewal. An estimated 76,000 jobs in 350 auto-related plants account for 22 percent of Kentucky's gross state income (A. Smith F1). Personal income derived from retail trade experienced an even greater increase, as did nearly all of the service sectors. The money spent by Toyota employees, circulating through Kentucky, created an estimated 26,374 additional Kentucky jobs.

Today even the incentives Collins offered Toyota to build water, sewer, and road access and to train Kentucky employees, all of which was spent in the state, have been recognized as an outstanding investment—returning almost three times more than that projected at the time. In return for the $147 million incentive package, Toyota promised a capital investment of $800 million, offering 3,000 jobs with an average annual employee income of $30,000, totaling an annual payroll of $90 million. In the ten years since they opened, Toyota has produced a capital investment five times greater than promised, hired two-and-one-half times as many employees, with an average annual employee income more than double that estimated and an annual payroll more than five times that promised. The return to the state on the incentive investment is calculated at more than 36 percent annually, or a total of $1.5 billion in tax revenues over twenty years (Haywood).

While considerable documentation confirms Collins' accomplishments, scant attention has been paid to how she achieved so much. In the bright light of her present acclaim, it would be easy to attribute the magnitude of Collins' influence to her dynamism, to her personal attractiveness, to her charisma. No doubt, external image contributed to her effectiveness, but the changes in Kentucky appear too significant and the battle too difficult to be neatly explained away by external image. No, Collins' rhetorical successes seem more related to the ways in which she views the world and herself.

External image alone would not likely have sustained Collins through the ridicule she suffered at the time she worked to create such dramatic change. For although her calls for education reform and economic development were popular with a large segment of the public, both required a startup fee. Education reform was estimated to require slightly more than $300 million and the incentives offered to Toyota required nearly half that amount, $147 million. Kentucky unemployment stood at nearly 12 percent, having doubled from 1979 to 1983. The recession had emptied state coffers and a newly elected governor who had campaigned on the promise of not increasing taxes immediately faced doing so.

Typical of someone who views events through the political frame, Collins attributed much of her administration's success at locating plants in Kentucky to the fact that she had assembled an economic development team that included cabinet-level people rather than those in project-level positions. As soon as a prospect had a question, they had an answer. Collins and her team had initiated contact with Toyota Motor Manufacturing in Japan in March 1985 before that company had even made any public announcement of their plans to open a plant in the United States. Her story of attracting the Toyota Motor Manufacturing plant to Scott County, Kentucky, also evidenced Collins' ability to transcend cultural limitations. She looked for and found common symbolic threads that provided the framework for shared meaning.

Collins framed events through the symbolic and political perspectives and, thus, allowed for a mutual identification with sufficient strength to overcome gender and cultural differences and to create change. Her efforts in both economic development and education reform went beyond compliance gaining. They went beyond impression management. Relying heavily on the symbolic and political frames, she developed a shared meaning with followers—at all levels, whether they were legislators, citizens of Kentucky, foreign manufacturers, or government and education officials—about the changes desired "for Kentucky" in the future. While Collins displayed charisma, her behavior exceeded magnetism based on good looks or an appealing public image. Rather, the explanation for Collins' influence lies *within* her. By cognitively framing and re-framing events and issues, Collins constructed a vision "for Kentucky" that allowed legislators and constituents both to share in that meaning.

Collins conceived of new opportunities for Kentucky, and in a simple and concrete way she framed those opportunities for others to see. In short, educator Martha Layne Collins—despite the economy, despite her gender—created change by educating others to view issues and events in a different way. These findings agree with Harry Broudy's observation that the frames serve as stencils and that the highest order of learning involves the development of stencils that give meaning to experience (cited in Bolman and Deal 19). These findings also bear out the frequently expressed hypothesis that leaders change both the perspectives and experience of others by re-framing. They do not make significant and lasting change without the active participation of the follower.

This analysis calls into question any notion that framing is both the act of defining an event and the assertion of that definition. It is highly unlikely that such behavior, whether exhibited by Cézanne or by Collins, would result in change of personally held perspectives. Rather, the leader and the follower in this instance seemed to define the meaning together. In the examples presented here, Collins did not paint a sunset as only she saw it. She did not dictate a plan; rather, she continuously connected with legislators, with the citizens of every small town, farm, and city in the state, and with foreign manufacturers to share her desires "for Kentucky." She wanted better education "for Kentucky." She wanted better jobs "for Kentucky." Artistlike, Collins painted a brighter future "for Kentucky." Unlike Cézanne, however, she encouraged others to paint that picture with her.

Chapter Five

The Fusion of Populist and Feminine Styles in the Rhetoric of Ann Richards

Shannon Skarphol Kaml

Ann Richards has been described as a Texas Treasure. As the governor of Texas, she came across as a female version of a Texas good ol' boy with a solicitous side, tempering her toughness with a genuine sense of caring for her constituents. Her speech, typically peppered with Texan colloquialisms and stories, produced a galvanic effect that transcended the self-depreciating humor she employed. Richards' rhetoric, a fusion of feminine and Populist style, helped her to become an enormously popular politician in a state where female political leaders are rare. This chapter examines the junctures where feminine style and Populist style converge and theorizes that the similarities are based on the commonality of circumstances of the original members of the early woman's rights movement and the Populist movement.

In order to see Richards' rhetoric as partaking equally of both traditions, I characterize feminine style and Populist style and examine elements of these styles in her rhetoric. Bonnie J. Dow notes that Richards' rhetoric is remarkably consistent in its tone and in the themes that it addresses ("Ann" 456). Therefore, following the example of Dow and Mari Boor Tonn in their analysis of Richards, her "Keynote Address" to the 1988 Democratic National Convention will serve as the primary text. Material from Richards' January 1991 Inaugural Address and her first State of the State Address to the Texas Legislature in February 1991 will be used to further validate these claims and to offer proof of the consistency of her style.

FEMININE STYLE

The concept of a "feminine style" derives from Campbell's analysis of the rhetoric of the early woman's rights movement. Because nineteenth-century society insisted that a woman's place was in the home, it subsequently developed strictures against women speaking in public. A powerful force in this restriction was the development of the Cult of True Womanhood, which demanded that all women be pure, pious, domestic, and submissive, qualities that practically prevented them from leaving the home to venture into a public sphere filled with enticements to immorality (Welter 21). Public speaking therefore came to be seen as a solely masculine activity, one that required traits that were unbecoming to a woman.

When women felt morally obligated to speak against slavery in the 1830s, they faced attacks both from their audience members and from the very religious institutions from which they derived their abolitionist beliefs. In July 1837, the General Association of the Massachusetts Congregational Church issued a Pastoral Letter warning against the impropriety and resulting moral degradation that occurred when women dared to take on the role of public reformers (Campbell, *Man* 1: 24). A woman's public speaking activities became even more problematic when she addressed promiscuous or mixed-sex audiences. Susan Zaeske delineates the changing meaning of the term "promiscuous" from an adjective used to denote simply "mixed" audiences to a declaration of a woman's licentious character (192–196). Most often the earliest addresses by females to promiscuous audiences were not sought by the women speakers involved but rather resulted from the popularity of their messages or the sheer novelty of hearing a woman speak in public. A notable exception was Frances Wright, a Scottish-born female speaker who spoke publicly for the Working Man's Party and championed a wide range of social reforms including abolition, woman's rights, and a republican system of education. In a number of instances, men actually attended women-only parlor talks held in private homes to witness women speakers of note, thereby creating the promiscuous-audience charge (Campbell, *Man* 1: 24).

Because of this prohibition against women speaking, the speakers of the early woman's rights movement developed rhetorical strategies designed to legitimate their right to speak and feminize the activity, thus minimizing the negative connotations of their actions. However, to be perceived as credible and competent by an audience, women still had to demonstrate their expertise, authority, and rationality, traits viewed as masculine by society at that time. Feminine style developed out of this double bind. Campbell characterizes the rhetoric of these women as: personal in tone; relying heavily on personal experience, anecdotes, and other examples as evidence; working from specific examples to general principles; inviting audience participation as a means of testing the speaker's conclusions and creating identification with the speaker; and the addressing of audience members as peers and equals, with recognition of authority based on experience (13). The goal of this type of rhetoric was the empowerment of other women. Dow and Boor Tonn argue that "the similarity between characteristics of woman's private world of experience and feminine style made the latter particularly effective for powerless female audiences" (288). Encouraged by the words of others, women were more able to see themselves as agents of change who could work for woman's rights.

Campbell argues that the feminine adaptation of rhetoric was similar to the way these women learned and practiced the crafts that comprised their lives. She writes:

Deprived of formal education and confined to the home, a woman learned the crafts of housewifery and motherhood—cooking, cleaning, canning, sewing, childbearing, child-rearing, and the like—from other women through a supervised internship combining expert advice with trial and error. (*Man* 1: 13)

Because rhetoric too can be understood as a craft, women's acquisition of rhetorical abilities followed the process by which they developed their other skills. Mentoring and imitation of role models played significant roles in the development of individual women's rhetorical competencies. This process prized the personal and concrete over the abstract and encouraged speakers who sought to empower their audiences to use inductive forms of logic and audience participation as means to foster the rhetorical skills of others. Campbell argues that the craftlike nature of rhetoric gives rise to a certain style of address when implemented by people previously skilled in the acquisition of crafts (*Man* 1: 13). This is feminine style.

Mentoring and mothering were familiar social roles for women in the 1800s. These roles often served as the justification for women's rhetorical activities. Advocates for woman's rights mixed appeals to women's special roles as moralizers and mothers with appeals to the law of natural rights and its core tenet that all humans have equal and inalienable rights. Although few feminists continue to promote women's moral superiority to men, this was the stance functioning implicitly in the Cult of True Womanhood. Campbell notes that because women were isolated and, hence, protected from the public sphere, they were perceived to have a heightened moral sensibility (*Man* 1: 10). The "Ministering Angel" of the home was responsible for the spiritual needs of the family and by extension of this notion morally obligated to promote a moral society.

Such early female abolitionist speakers as the Grimké sisters and Lucretia Mott were aware of the bind created by their simultaneous dedication to a moral obligation and adherence to proper womanly upbringing. They explicitly developed arguments based on women's superior morality and used biblical examples of female leaders to enable their speaking while preserving their womanliness (Zaeske 199–202). During her May 16, 1838, Address at Pennsylvania Hall, Angelina Grimké took the moral arguments she had developed previously to their logical conclusion by enacting the role of a prophetess (Campbell, *Man* 1: 30). In this unusual example of early female rhetoric, Grimké turns the screams of the angry crowd gathered outside the hall in which she spoke to her own advantage as living proofs of the immorality of those who supported slavery. The burning of the hall the next evening serves as further proof of the effectiveness of the moral education she provided. Moral uplift became the justification that later women activists used to advocate their political programs. The rhetoric of Frances Willard, who sponsored temperance and woman's suffrage, and of Jane Addams, who founded Hull House in Chicago, provide many examples of the theme of woman as moralizer.

Mothering also entails a certain component in moral education, as mothers are expected to train their children in appropriate types of behavior. Numerous speakers for the early woman's rights movement relied on their roles and needs as mothers to justify the necessity for social change and their right to speak. Themes that traverse the rhetoric of Elizabeth Cady Stanton, Ernestine Potowski Rose, and Clarina Howard Nichols include: the abuse and neglect of children by their fathers, the obligation to educate mothers to raise educated children, and the necessity for property and divorce laws to enable women to be better wives and mothers.

The explicit adoption of the persona of a mother is a powerful rhetorical device used by later women speakers. Mari Boor Tonn has illustrated that the unique blend of mothering's feminine and authoritative characteristics made "Mother" an ideal persona for female union agitators like Mary Harris "Mother" Jones. "Mothering is a diverse and complex practice, to be sure. Nonetheless, most mothers of all stripes appear to share three general goals: securing their children's physical survival, furthering their emotional and intellectual growth and independence, and cultivating their connection and accountability to their social group" (Tonn 4).

Although Boor Tonn acknowledges that the physical survival of offspring is a motherly concern that has been alleviated for the most part in the Western world, the ethic of care embedded in mothering legitimates protection of those younger or less able. A mother's ethic of care makes social criticism rhetorically possible, perhaps even morally necessary, and yet still preserves a feminine persona. Feminine style is appropriate to the project of raising children, since "many mothers interact with their children in ways that mirror important aspects of what Campbell has termed 'feminine' style, a rhetorical technique with similar consciousness-raising efforts used in movements for purposes of mobilization" (Tonn 8).

Some contemporary feminine rhetoric still utilizes the themes of mothering and moralizing for its rhetorical force and does so in an explicitly feminine style. Dow and Boor Tonn have argued that "these characteristics [of feminine style] hold true in some contemporary discourse because, while the historical conditions of women have changed in many ways, their primary social roles have not" (287). Although working outside the home has become an economic necessity, women are still expected to be full-time mothers and wives in addition to their jobs in the public sphere. They further extend their analysis by claiming that a feminine style of speech has become entrenched in society. As such, even when the crafts of housewifery and motherhood are absent from a woman's life, women in U.S. society are encouraged to use feminine modes of communication, which are concrete, participatory, cooperative, and oriented toward relationship maintenance (288).

FEMININE STYLE IN THE RHETORIC OF ANN RICHARDS

Dow and Boor Tonn indicate that the rhetoric of Ann Richards is one example of the use of feminine style. They "suggest that the most useful way to understand the appeal of her discourse is as a manifestation of contemporary feminine style" (289). They also point out that "the dominance of personal anecdotes, concrete examples, and brief narratives in Richards' 1988 address to the Democratic National Convention is perhaps the most visible hallmark of feminine style" (289). Other markers of what Campbell originally referred to as feminine style are apparent in Richards' rhetoric as well. Richards is typically very personal in her tone, she reasons from specific examples to general principles, she invites audience participation as a means of testing her conclusions and creating identification with her as a speaker, and she addresses audience members as peers and equals, with recognition of authority based on experience. Empowerment of voters or her constituents is explicitly Richards' goal in many of her addresses. Although Richards began her speaking career almost 150 years after the first well-known women speakers in the United States had claimed the public platform, it is interesting to note that references to mothering and numerous implicit examples of moralizing are present in her political rhetoric as well.

As Dow and Boor Tonn observed, Richards' speeches are full of concrete examples. Through the use of an unusual rhetorical device, the frame of a history textbook, Richards makes her Inaugural Address concrete:

Twenty, fifty, one hundred years from now, school children will open their textbooks—or perhaps, switch on their video texts—and they will see a picture.

They will see us standing proudly on this bright winter noon. And looking through the eyes of a child we will seem as distant and ancient as portraits of our ancestors seem to us.

Those children will read that on January 15th, 1991, a woman named Ann W. Richards took the oath of office as the 45th Governor of Texas. ("Remarks" 1–2)

Similarly, Richards relates the story of the gift of a beekeeper by using specific details in her State of the State Address:

When I moved into the Governor's Mansion the other day, I found a gallon of honey waiting for me. Attached to it was a hand-written note on a scrap of paper.

The hand that wrote the note was old and shaky. It was written by a man who worked hard all his life but didn't mind sharing some of the fruits of his hard labor.

The note said, "We believe we finally have a governor who cares about the ordinary people and the poor." ("Remarks" 10)

Richards strives to make both her longer anecdotes and shorter descriptions tangible to her audience. In one sentence from her keynote speech, Richards reminds her audience to consider all of the Republicans so-called debacles of the preceding eight years: "In a little more than 100 days the Reagan-Meese-Deaver-Nofziger-Poindexter-North-Weinberger-Watt-Gorsuch-Lavelle-Stockman-Haig-Bork-Noriega-George Bush era will be over" (1). By using the names associated with each incident, Richards asks her audience to complete the enthymeme and conjure up specific information about each scandal.

Personal anecdotes are sprinkled liberally throughout her speeches. Only seconds into her keynote, Richards describes a story from her youth to her audience: "You know, tonight I feel like I did when I played basketball in the eighth grade. I thought I looked real cute in my uniform and then I heard a boy yell from the bleachers, 'Make a basket, bird legs'" (1). This self-disclosure helps personalize her as a speaker and undercuts the acerbic humor of her preceding comments about women doing everything men can even when they do it with the additional handicaps of wearing high heels and following men's leads. Richards also refers to her humble beginnings during the Depression, when she listened to people talk about politics on summer nights as she lay on a Baptist pallet. Through her use of personal anecdotes, Richards helps her audiences see her as one of them; this basis of shared experience adds to the persuasive effect of her message.

Richards' rhetoric also includes personal references to her roles as mother and grandmother. Boor Tonn indicates that the tradition of having wise women and grandmothers pass down sage advice through the telling of stories and myths is a privilege of motherhood. Richards utilizes this tradition as she informs the audience that she will tell her granddaughter, Lilly, about the Democratic triumphs she witnessed during her lifetime (4). Richards also validates the real-life stories of other mothers in the United States when she reads a letter from a mother in Lorena, Texas, during her address to the Democratic National Convention:

Our worries go from payday to payday, just like millions of others, and we have two fairly decent incomes. But I worry about how I'm going to pay the rising car insurance and food. I pray my kids don't have a growth spurt from August to December so I don't have to buy new jeans. We buy clothes at the budget stores and have them fray, and fade, and stretch in the first wash. We ponder and try to figure out how we're going to pay for college, and braces, and tennis shoes. We don't take vacations and we don't go out to eat. ("Keynote" 2)

Richards' use of self-disclosure within the themes of motherhood and mothering further invites audience identification with her. This creation of positive identification with the audience is another prominent feature of feminine style.

In keeping with the numerous instances of self-disclosure that Richards provides as concrete examples, her rhetoric is also highly personal in tone. She treats her audiences as groups of peers. This helps create further identification with her audience. She directly addresses her audience at the Democratic National Convention, often referring to them with the informal "you" and as "my friends." She often includes herself as one of the members of the group that the audience represents by using the inclusive pronoun *we*. Likewise, in her Inaugural Address, Richards includes her audience's participation in her plan for a New Texas by the repetition of the phrase "Tomorrow we must build that Texas" ("Remarks" 2). Her State of the State Address also attempts to include the audience. While outlining her goals, Richards says, "We're going to be progressive in this administration. . . . We will be active, alert. . . . Together, we will be working to build a New Texas" ("State" 1).

Richards displays feminine style also by inviting audience participation in the formation of her claims. By basing her political judgments on standards that everyone can understand and implement, such as personal experience and practical wisdom, Richards allows the audience to participate directly in this process (Dow and Boor Tonn 290). In her "Keynote Address," Richards encourages audience participation first by validating their feelings. She says, "Well of course you believe you're forgotten. Because you have been" (2). This validation is the start of the process whereby she encourages the audience members to trust in their own feelings as a basis for judging government. As Boor Tonn notes, this process is nearly identical with the manner in which many mothers encourage autonomy in their children (8).

In this same speech, Richards further encourages her audience to use their own experience in determining the truth of Republican claims. "They tell us employment rates are great and they're for equal opportunity, but we know it takes two paychecks to make ends meet today, when it used to take one" ("Keynote" 4). Likewise, she encourages her audience to judge governments as they would judge individuals and insist that government officials be consistent in their words and deeds: "They tell us, they are fighting a war against terrorists. And then we find that the White House is selling arms to the Ayatollah. They tell us they're fighting a war on drugs, then people come on TV and testify that the CIA, and the DEA, and the FBI knew they were flying drugs into America all along" ("Keynote" 3).

Richards further privileges personal experience as a means of political judgment by advocating that the same skills people use as parents can be useful in judging governments. When referring to Reagan and the Iran-Contra Affair, she says, "the only answer we get is, 'I don't know,' or 'I forgot.' But you wouldn't accept that answer from your children. I wouldn't. Don't tell me 'you don't know' or 'you forgot' " ("Keynote" 3).

These examples also demonstrate Richards' use of inductive reasoning, another characteristic of feminine style. She gives her audience numerous examples of the Republican Party's behavior while in power and then draws a general conclusion about the party on the basis of these examples. By following these links in her chain of reasoning, audience members should be led to the same conclusion that Richards reaches. She claims the Republicans have treated Americans like special interest groups, that they are out of touch with the common person, and that they have lied to us. Moral judgments about the proper conduct of government officials are implicit in Richards' chain of reasoning. In contrast to the lies and deceit of the Republicans, her claim in the introduction that "we're going to tell how the cow ate the cabbage" is an implied reference to the truthfulness of her statements

("Keynote" 1). Richards makes her moral judgments more explicit at other points in her Democratic National Convention Address. Her repetition of the phrases "that's wrong" and "they're wrong" after the various claims the Republicans have asserted is indicative of her moral stance. In one example, she says, "they told working mothers it's all their fault that families are falling apart—because they had to go to work to keep their kids in jeans, tennis shoes and college. And they're wrong" ("Keynote" 2). This moral dimension of her address is similar to the moral education mothers are expected to provide their children. Although Richards does not explicitly argue in support of her apparent heightened moral sensibility or superior moral reasoning, these claims function among the methods she uses to empower her audience.

Dow and Boor Tonn argue that Richards' use of a nurturing persona fosters growth in others toward a greater capacity for independent action (Dow and Boor Tonn 296–297). Through enactment Richards shows her audience a new method of evaluating government. She reassures the average people that they can make political judgments themselves and that they don't need to wait for the political analysts to tell them how to vote. Creating agents of change is part of Richards' purpose in her Democratic National Convention Address. After summing up the experiences of the common person under the Reagan administration, she says, "Nothing's wrong with you that you can't fix in November" ("Keynote" 3).

Empowerment, too, is a fundamental aspect of feminine style "because the generalizations reached from validation of personal experience lead to the realization that the 'personal is political,' a process which produces group cohesion and transforms audience members into 'agents of change' " (Dow and Boor Tonn 289). Richards also uses a nurturing persona in her gubernatorial addresses to foster her audience's sense of empowerment: "Because when my time in office is finished, I want us to be able to look back together and say we—not he, not she, not me—but WE came to this moment with a vision worthy of great heritage. . . . and WE realized that vision in a way that was worthy of a great future" ("Remarks" 3).

Similarly, Richards used this nurturing persona in her State of the State Address to encourage and empower the members of the Texas legislature. She shares a bit of personal experience with them in the following statement: "Sam Rayburn, a great Texan who sat where Speaker Lewis now sits, said something to me one time that I think applies to us. He said, 'There's no limit to the good you can accomplish if you don't care who gets the credit.' And I don't care" (10). In this quotation, Richards, like any mother, claims that she doesn't want the credit, she merely wants "her offspring," the legislature, to do the work.

The rhetoric of former Texas governor Ann Richards is clearly an example of the feminine style identified by Campbell. Richards exhibits all the traits generally associated with feminine style: a personal tone, use of personal experience and anecdotes, address of the audience as peers, attempts at creating identification with her audience, inductive logic, the recognition of authority that is based on experience, and the creation of empowerment. But as Dow and Boor Tonn imply in their comment, "Richards' Texas background clearly is reflected in her rhetoric," Richards' discourse is more than just a contemporary exemplar of feminine style (289); her rhetoric exemplifies Populist style as well.

To better understand what Populist oratory is and to test the validity of this claim, I now turn to a description of the characteristics of Populist rhetoric. Although a number of people, including Thomas R. Burkholder and David H. Ecroyd, recently have studied the rhetoric of the Populist movement, none of them appear to have comprehensively outlined the elements of Populist style. Ecroyd comes close to defining a Populist style of rhetoric when he describes three common features of this brand of oratory. He identifies reliance on factual materials that were essentially common knowledge, the merger of this factual material with emotional appeals, and adaptation to the audience as essential features of Populist rhetoric (Ecroyd 178–179). However, this analysis of Populist rhetoric does little to describe how Populist speakers actually marshaled their facts, designed their emotional appeals, or adapted to their audiences. In order to facilitate this study, more specific characteristics of a Populist style must first be derived from the rhetoric of the movement. To more fully understand and describe this type of discourse, I will examine some basic background information about the movement, its speakers, and its aims.

THE ORIGINS OF POPULISM AND A POPULIST STYLE

Populism was a social movement that sprang up during the later half of the nineteenth century primarily because of the common person's discontent with his financial prospects. The structure of society was changing rapidly in the late 1880s; many were unwilling to accept this change because they failed to see that it was to their advantage to do so. Some people wanted to return to the "good ol' days," while others looked to the government for reforms that would protect them from being exploited by "big business." Fraternal organizations and labor unions emerged out of this feeling of desperation and provided a support network for their members that helped to boost morale. The Knights of Labor and the Farmers' Alliance were two such groups that eventually served as the basis for the People's Party, a third party seeking political solutions for perceived social ills. It is interesting to note that both of these organizations were pioneers in the area of women's participation in pressure groups. At the same time that women were being excluded entirely or forced to join special "women only" branches of many of the other fraternal organizations, the Farmers' Alliance welcomed the participation of women on a nearly equal basis with men. This tradition carried on in the People's Party and "to a larger extent than either of the conventional parties the Peoples' Party included women in their leadership and campaigning" (Boardman 30). In some western U.S. states, the People's Party carried this idea to its logical conclusion and advocated woman's suffrage (Burkholder, "Kansas" 299).

The Farmers' Alliance came to dominate the People's Party, and most of the organization's notable speakers got their start stumping and lecturing at Alliance meetings. According to Lawrence Goodwyn, Populism adopted its motto, "Equal rights for all and special privileges for none," at the 1892 Omaha convention (*vii*). The clear development of party ideology and the superior organizational training of the Farmers' Alliance members are two reasons for the prominence of western, agrarian-based rhetoric in the rhetoric of the Peoples' Party. Historically, the label "Populist rhetoric" refers to the speeches of the agrarian half of the Peoples' Party because these speakers were the most prominent campaigners.

The ability to persuade and entertain audiences as political speakers were expected to do in the 1800s was so important to the members of the Farmers' Alliance that they established training programs for speakers: "Through training Alliance people grew accustomed to discussing, debating, and lecturing as parts of their own lives, for every group held panels, debates, and other 'speakings' regularly" (Ecroyd 177). To aid these rhetorical efforts, the Farmers' Alliance printed informational pamphlets on their political positions and "sourcebooks" for speakers containing quotations from the political speeches of other parties (Ecroyd 178). As a result of the nearly uniform training they received and the rather limited information they had to use as the basis for their speeches, Populists speakers were often remarkably similar to one another in content and style. When it was alleged that one notable speaker had stolen a story from another speaker, the reply usually was "I put the quotation marks in, but you couldn't hear them" (Ecroyd 178).

Populist rhetoric is more homogeneous than the rhetoric of many social movements because of its agrarian roots and the program of rhetorical training that many of its speakers underwent. Although it is difficult and dangerous to generalize about any group, and particularly one so numerous as the Populists speakers, I delineated some of the common trademarks of the rhetoric of these Western speakers in a previous analysis (Skarphol Kaml). Populist style consists of a varied tone, ranging from accusatory to laudatory but predominately personal, utilizing a conversational style based on the direct address of the audience as peers and equals; creation of identification with the audience and enhancement of the speakers' ethos through the use of common knowledge and the reflection of common experiences in the form of personal examples and anecdotes as well as factual materials contained in Farmers' Alliance pamphlets and newspapers; and the creation of empowerment by a privileging of the experience and wisdom of the common person over other segments of society, by encouraging the listeners to participate in the testing of claims, by appeals to their unique patriotic and moral virtues and by the creation of a common enemy. As indicated above, describing a Populist style is difficult because a central element of the rhetoric, the use of common knowledge and experience, functions in so many ways. The following brief analysis of Populist style will focus on the two key functions of the rhetoric, identification and empowerment, to further illuminate common elements of Populist style.

Populist orators often addressed groups of people who knew about economic hardships both from their own lives and from witnessing the lives of their neighbors. Populist rhetors often appealed to these sentiments by articulating the feelings of their audiences, by sharing their experiences. J. L. Hammers said, "to prove that there is a financial depression among the laboring classes of this country one only needs to look around him." He continued, "here we see the rich growing richer and the poor growing poorer. Here we see through 'class legislation' the wealth of the many congregating into the hands of the few" (qtd. in Burkholder, "Mythic" 297). Many in the late 1800s were disaffected with government. Mary Lease, a prominent Populist orator who spoke nationally for the People's Party, used an appeal to American ideals while stating the obvious for her audience. She summed the situation up as follows: "It is no longer a government of the people, by the people and for the people, but a government of Wall Street, by Wall Street and for Wall Street" (qtd. in Burkholder, "Mary" 114). These examples from typical Populist rhetoric illustrate how frequently the Populist speaker uses reflection of common beliefs.

By articulating the audiences' beliefs and grievances, Populist rhetors created identification with their audiences of the most fundamental sort. This is Kenneth Burke's concept of material identification. This type of identification has been appropriately described as "the politician who, addressing an audience of farmers, says 'I was a farm boy myself' " (Burke, *Rhetoric* xiv). Also, Populist orators built their own ethos and credibility by convincing their audiences that they were members of the group. This identification was further strengthened by the fact that the speaker often actually was one of the people. Because of the Farmers' Alliance program of rhetorical training and its insistence that anyone could get up at one of their meetings and make a speech, farmers and their wives addressed other members of their communities in public ways not previously possible (Ecroyd 177). Unlike the rhetoric of many social movements that attempts to persuade people to join or support the movement, Populist rhetoric was not aimed at converting the audience or even ostensibly educating them about the Populist cause. Instead, its rhetoric served more of a cathartic purpose, confirming what the audience already knew or believed to be true. In doing so, it encouraged the audience to participate in the testing of the speakers' claims by comparing the experiences described by the speakers to their own experiences.

Examples demonstrating the use of common knowledge and personal experience in Populist rhetoric also show how the Populist rhetors used a personal tone based on a conversational style and addressed their audiences as peers. Populist discourse is not the flowery and ornate rhetoric typical of the nineteenth century, but instead it cuts straight to the point. In fact, Populist orators often encouraged one another to use "simplicity of style and clarity of organization" in their speeches (Ecroyd 177). Frequent use of the inclusive pronoun *we* bridged the gap between the speaker and the audience. In this manner, Populist speakers created an audience of peers, people who were seen to be equally capable of reaching the conclusions that the speaker had drawn. Use of group identification further encouraged audience members to test the speaker's claims and conclusions.

Empowerment is a second key function of Populist rhetoric. Populist rhetors emphasized the special qualities of the farmer and laborer as a means to encourage them to participate in the movement and as a means to persuade them that they were capable of effecting the needed change in the government. According to Populist rhetoric, only the heroic, patriotic, morally pure members of society could promote the needed change for the betterment of all the citizens of the United States. The speeches of Lease and others provide many examples of the way the Populist orator privileged the common person and his experiences. Lease claimed:

The farmers in every great conflict that has swept this country from the battle of Lexington down to the great rebellion have always come to the front and have solved the great questions involved successfully. Today they are called to solve the labor question. You may club down the laborers in the cities and make them slaves of plutocracy, but you cannot, thank God! starve and club down the farmers of this country who stand ready to save it. (qtd. in Burkholder, "Kansas" 297)

Populist rhetor Mrs. J. T. Whitman echoed Lease by saying that "the industrial and agricultural classes of society are the real foundations of our government and the support of our institutions has been taught us from our earliest recollections" (Burkholder, "Kansas" 296). Populist speakers also appealed to the common person's religious sensibilities and patriotic zeal when attempting to empower their audiences and encourage political action. Lease declared:

The moral conscience has been quickened, the heart of the nation aroused, and we are asking, in all earnestness, "with malice toward none and charity for all," which of the political parties can best solve the problems of the day? And we answer unhesitatingly, that party which is most in accord with the teachings of Christ. (qtd. in Ecroyd 181)

She even went so far as to say, "If you vote for any other party you vote for a hell on earth" (qtd. in Burkholder, "Mary" 116). Other Populist rhetors combined patriotic appeals with religious appeals as a means of inspiring the audience. M. W. Cobun wrote:

I do not believe the time has yet come when people will submit to the rule of tyrants. I believe the patriotic spirit of '76 is again being re-kindled in the hearts of the people. I believe universal liberty will again sweep over this entire country with plutocratic despotism chained to her chariot wheels.

But one thing we should not forget is that God reigns. We should take God into our politics. (qtd. in Ecroyd 182)

Kansas Senator William Peffer made a straight appeal to patriotic virtues when he said: "Then let all of us, every man whose work adds anything to the wealth of the country, or to the comfort of the people, unite in this movement, with malice toward none, but with charity to all, gathering force as you go along" (qtd. in Burkholder, "Kansas" 296). He further empowered his audience by proclaiming that they would "sweep the country like a cyclone sweeps our western prairies" (297).

Finding a scapegoat for the plight of the common people provided an additional source of empowerment in Populist rhetoric. Mentions of "tyrants" and "plutocrats" run rampant in Populist oratory. Unfaltering references to the graft and corruption of big business and the government are also commonplace. However, unlike the monopolist and the industrialist, who were directly blamed for the unequal distribution of wealth, the common laborer was never blamed for his situation. The common people were never told that it was their own laziness that caused their poverty or that it was their previous inaction that had allowed the industrialists and bankers to take over the country. Instead, they were told that the situation was unfair and that the cause was outside their realm of individual action. By removing the cause of the situation from the common people's realm of influence, Populist rhetors absolved their audiences of blame and stirred up their hatred for the moneyed class. Lorenzo D. Lewelling, the Populist governor of Kansas, set up a simple standard to absolve the common person of blame. He said:

Now I am going to say something to you, whether you are a merchant, whether you are a business man or a farmer or a day-laborer, it is my opinion that if you are an honest and industrious citizen; if you are frugal, if you are careful of what you earn, that you have the right to enough to eat and drink, and clothe your self and family, and if you do not have it, it is because somebody else has got more than his fair share. (qtd. in Burkholder, "Kansas" 297)

By placing the source of blame well outside the common person's sphere of influence, the Populist rhetor also created a need for the people to turn to government for relief. But because rhetors painted the current members of government as involved in a conspiracy with members of business, the common person was encouraged to work for reform within the confines of the People's Party. This approach justified third-party political action. A consequence of scapegoating and a further hallmark of Populist style are the extreme changes of tone that a Populist rhetor used when praising the common person and attacking the wealthy.

POPULIST STYLE IN THE RHETORIC OF ANN RICHARDS

The Farmers' Alliance and the Grange that preceded it were particularly active in the southern and western regions of the United States. Texas, Ann Richards' home state, was once firmly enmeshed in Populism, and its unique culture still reflects the individualism inherent in Populist ideals. It is no small coincidence then that Richards' rhetoric is thoroughly flecked with touches of both Populist and feminine style.

As noted previously, Richards consistently uses a personal tone and addresses her audience as peers and equals, both traits of Populist and feminine styles. Like the Populist rhetors before her, Richards makes great efforts to build identification with her audience, particularly by rehearsing their feelings for them. Richards' statements in her keynote speech that the Republicans had forgotten the people is a powerful example, as is her use of the letter from the mother in Lorena. She does this in a milder form in her first State of the State Address in Texas. In this address, which was given directly to the Texas Legislature, broadcast on local channels, and covered in the news, she tells the members of the legislature about the common person's experience with Texas government:

In a New Texas there will be no doubt in the people's minds that this government is here to serve the people. It is hardly a radical notion—Thomas Jefferson would have understood it—but it is one that many of our fellow Texans have grown skeptical about. With good reason.

They are suspicious about our motives, yours and mine. They are distressed about the seductive smell of money in the political process and the influence of narrow special interests. Sit in a barbershop some afternoon or on the stool of a small town drugstore counter and listen to what the people say.

They hate the bureaucracy. They come to Austin looking for answers, for help, and what they get is the runaround. They get bounced from one office to another until their eyes blur and their feet give out. (1–2)

As discussed previously, Richards further creates identification by validating her audiences' feelings and by building shared experience through numerous references to the experiences she has in common with her audience.

Like the Populist speakers, Richards also relies almost entirely on common knowledge to further create identification with her audience. It is rare for her to give a heavily factual speech. Even her State of the State Address, which, like a president's State of the Union Address, could be expected to be highly factual, contains few real statistics and fewer yet that her immediate audience would not have known. Similarly, during her Democratic National Convention "Keynote Address," Richards relies heavily on common knowledge. She does not have to document the state of the economy for her audience; rather, she relies on a simple statement to accomplish this task: "Now they tell us that employment rates are great and that they're for equal opportunity, but we know it takes two paychecks to make ends meet today" ("Keynote" 4). By using examples everyone knew, Richards creates further identification and builds her ethos because she allows her audience to test the reasonableness of her conclusions themselves.

Richards' rhetoric, like Populist rhetoric, emphasizes the centrality of the ordinary person's role in government and privileges the experience of the ordinary person as a means of empowering that individual. This is seen explicitly, as discussed above, in the new standard that she creates for political judgment based on personal experience and practical wisdom. As Dow and Boor Tonn note, Richards "creates an implicit standard for political judgment that is based on the primacy of experiential knowledge and inductive reasoning; second it explicitly critiques the validity of standards that cannot meet this standard" (289). In other words, Richards actually advocates that a standard of political judgment based on personal experience and practical wisdom is better than the traditional standards of judgment, which rely on the analysis and opinions of academics and political analysts.

In emphasizing the importance of the common people and in attempting to empower them, Richards, like the Populist orators, appeals to the inherent nobility of the common person. Her speeches are full of tributes to the common person. In the conclusion of her Democratic National Convention Address, Richards says that she plans to tell her granddaughter "that for all our difference, we're still the greatest nation on this good earth. And our strength lies in the men and women who go to work every day, who struggle to balance their family and their jobs, and who should never, ever be forgotten ("Keynote" 6).

By honoring the struggles and the daily efforts of the common person, not the rich or the powerful, Richards inspires her audience to act. Like the Populists' numerous references to the valor and patriotism of the farmer, Richards makes her audience aware and proud of the role that they have played in shaping this country and challenges them to continue in this path.

As Dow notes in her analysis, Richards' rhetoric also implicitly buys into the Populist belief that the common person is the savior of government through its emphasis on the centrality of the common person's role in government ("Ann" 456). In her Inaugural Address, Richards proclaims, "Today, we marched up Congress Avenue and said that we were reclaiming the Capitol for the people of Texas. We say proudly the people of Texas are back" ("Remarks" 1). Like the Populist rhetors, Richards claims that the government should be run by the people. Likewise, she argues that there is something wrong with government if it does not serve the common person. She says, "We begin with the understanding that government must stop telling people what they want . . . and start listening to people and hearing what the people need" ("Remarks" 3). She reemphasizes this point in her first State of the State Address. "We are building a government that means something good in people's lives, a government that is going to make the lives of the ordinary Texans better" (10). In her inaugural speech, she focuses on the centrality of the common person in government by emphasizing her administration's stance: "Nothing is more fundamentally important to me than the understanding that this administration exists to *serve* . . . service to the people is government's bottom line" ("Remarks" 3).

The final aspect of Populist style that can be clearly seen in Richards' rhetoric is the creation of a common enemy as an additional means of empowerment. Dow comments, "She does not hesitate to attack political behavior that appears dishonest or counterproductive, and she encourages her audience to do the same" ("Ann" 462). This is most clearly evidenced by her

Democratic National Convention Address. Richards draws distinctions between good and bad political behavior in several ways in this address, the most significant being the creation of an "Us versus Them" mentality that portrays the Republicans as un-American. She claims, "This Republican administration treats us as if we were pieces of a puzzle that can't fit together" ("Keynote" 2). She then generalizes about the Republican political strategy from this concrete example and states, "Their political theory is divide and conquer" (2). Richards further vilifies the Republicans by blaming America's lack of cohesiveness on Republican policies: "We've been isolated. We've been lumped into the sad phraseology called 'special interests' " (2). This strategy of finding a scapegoat for society's problems is also consistent with Populist style. A further similarity between Richards' rhetoric and Populist rhetoric is the way she avoids blaming her audience for society's ills. She sees Americans as unwilling victims of Republican policies and urges them to fight back. "There's nothing wrong with you that you can't fix in November," she emphasizes (3).

Richards' constant use of the pronouns *they, them* and *their* in the above examples and throughout her speech further serves to define the Republicans as the enemy, or the "other." This is especially true when contrasted to the inclusive labels she uses to refer to the rest of American society. She paints all the non-Republicans as one homogeneous group. She repeatedly uses the phrases "we believe" and "we Democrats believe." This use of repetition also reflects a common strategy in Populist rhetoric. By echoing the preamble of the Declaration of Independence, Richards ties her statements to patriotic beliefs.

Following the example of the Populists, Richards also depicts her enemies as un-American. She contrasts Reagan's apparent proclivity to lie or forget during the Iran-Contra scandal with the truthfulness of Roosevelt, who, during the Depression, told the American people that they would have to make sacrifices to get the country back on its feet. In so doing, she emphasizes traits that have gone against the grain of Americanism since George Washington's administration. Richards also points out that Republican lying isn't solely isolated to Reagan when she demonstrates the contradictions between what the Republicans said their policies would accomplish and what they actually did. She compares numerous examples of the contradictory and counterproductive Republican policies to the classic Democratic policies that made people's lives better: "People in rural areas were told that we deserved to have electric lights, and they were going to harness the energy that was necessary to give us electricity so my grandmama didn't have to carry that old coal oil lamp around" ("Keynote" 5).

A second way Richards depicts the Republicans as un-American is by labeling them as a party of the privileged: "For eight straight years George Bush hasn't displayed the slightest interest in anything we care about. And now he's after a job that he can't get appointed to, he's like Columbus discovering America" ("Keynote" 4). Richards conveys the impression that Bush is a member of the elite and that he is so out of touch with America that he is unable to speak without committing some gaffe, and she refers to him as being "born with a silver foot in his mouth" (4). That the Republicans can be satisfied with the status quo is Richards' final argument that either the Republicans are better off than the rest of America or that they hold beliefs counter to the American ideal of progress. Richards offers her audience a distinct choice between the parties by stating, "So when it comes right down to it, this election is a contest between those who are satisfied with what they have—and those who know we can do better. That's what this election is really about. It's about the American dream. Those who want to keep it for the few—and those of us who know it must be nurtured and passed along" (6). Either way the audience interprets Richards' remark, it is the Republicans who look bad because they are seen as being against the common person's interests or as un-American.

SIMILARITIES BETWEEN FEMININE AND POPULIST STYLES IN RICHARDS' RHETORIC

As the preceding analysis indicates, Richards' rhetoric partakes of both Populist style and feminine style. Richards popularizes feminine style by making it stronger and more assertive and feminizes Populist style by making it less divisive and more cooperative (Dow, "Ann" 456). In this way, she proves that one can be both thoroughly feminine and Populist at the same time. As fascinating as this overlaying of styles is from a rhetorical perspective, what is most interesting in Richards' rhetoric is not her ability to use both of these styles but rather the fact that these styles are essentially a single style. A direct comparison of stylistic features will help illustrate this commonality (see Table 5.1).

Admittedly, there are some small differences between feminine style and Populist style. For instance, Populist rhetoric uses more variation in tone, ranging from a personal tone to both laudatory and accusatory tones. However, these differences are derived from the content of the rhetoric rather than actual stylistic differences. For example, depending on their subject matter, women speakers such as Angelina Grimké, Ernestine Potowski Rose, and Elizabeth Cady Stanton could be very strident in their tone, although they often used a personal tone when addressing their audiences.

Table 5.1
Comparison of Characteristics of Feminist and Populist Rhetorical Styles

Feminine Style	Populist Style
Personal Tone	Variation of Tone: Using Personal, Laudatory and Accusatory Tones
Address of Audience as Peers	Address of Audience as Peers
Audience Involvement Encouraged in Testing Claims	Audience Involvement Encouraged in Testing Claims
Creation of Identification	Creation of Identification
Use of Personal Experience, Anecdotes, and Concrete Examples	Use of Common Knowledge, Reflection of Common Experience through Use of Personal Experience, Examples and Anecdotes
Inductive Structure	Inductive and Deductive Structure
Recognition of Authority Based on Experience	Recognition of Authority of Common Person
Empowerment as a Goal	Empowerment as a Goal

Likewise, Populist rhetors divided society into two large classes, the workers and the industrialists, and varied their tone according to the class they were referring to at the time. However, Populist orators, like the speakers of the early woman's rights movement, often used a personal tone.

The similarity between feminine style and Populist style can be explained in a number of ways. The first reason for the similarity of feminine and Populist styles stems from the fact that both models were largely developed in social movements. Many of the speakers for the early woman's rights movement were first members of the abolitionist movement and gradually developed their own social movement based singularly on the advocacy of woman's rights. Likewise, the members of the Farmers' Alliance rapidly organized themselves into a social movement advocating reform and then into a political party. Using the seven elements of a social movement characterized throughout Neil Smelser's *Theory of Collective Behavior*—membership, structural strain, a precipitating event, organization, leadership, ideology, and opposition—we can identify numerous places where rhetoric would be necessary and influential in a social movement. Speakers for any social movement, then, can be seen as serving many important and similar rhetorical functions.

For the speakers of the early woman's rights movement and the Populist movement, the need to attract and maintain a sizable membership helps to create similarities in rhetorical style. This is at least partially true because the rhetorical concepts of identification and empowerment become essential for maintaining and attracting members to any cause. Creation of identification is crucial in a social movement because members must feel that they have some common cause or bond to continue to support the specific movement. Positive identification between speaker and audience member was more crucial in both the early woman's rights movement and the Populist movement than in a number of other social movements because both had to appeal to diverse groups for their support. Developing a sense of empowerment is fundamental to social movement rhetoric because members will not remain active in the movement unless they believe they can actually effect change in society. The numerous failures that both the Populists and the early feminists experienced made empowerment an essential feature of their discourse.

The similar ways in which the advocates of early woman's rights and the Populist rhetors created identification and empowerment stem potentially from their common backgrounds. This idea provides us with the second potential reason for the similarity of Populist style and feminine style. Both the early feminists and the Populists were groups of people who received little official education but were instead highly adept at learning crafts and familiar with the mentoring process that accompanied this activity. Farming, like housewifery, consists of a series of skills that are learned when young and perfected throughout a lifetime of trial and error. Tilling, planting, cultivating, and harvesting all have their natural rhythms that vary from place to place and season to season. Additionally, farmers in the nineteenth century learned a whole host of craftlike skills to support their primary vocation. Blacksmithing, carpentry, and animal husbandry were all essential skills for isolated prairie farmers. Along a similar vein, the Populists also learned to speak in a manner much like that of the speakers for the early woman's rights movement. Numerous eloquent spokespersons for both movements developed their speaking skills by following the examples others presented.

Although born well after the Populist and woman's rights movements had run their courses, Richards shares many similarities with members of these earlier groups. Her early experiences, which were filled with frugality and craft-learning, are similar to those of early woman's rights advocates or Populists, whereas her current socioeconomic status and well-rounded educational background are similar to the qualities of some of the leaders of these groups. Ann Willis, an only child, grew up during the Depression in

Lakeville, Texas, a pin-dot town outside of Waco. She struggled to meet the high expectations placed on her by a pair of rural Texas parents who had grown up on dirt-poor farms outside the even smaller towns of Bugtussle and Hogjaw. Like many of the Populists before her, Richards was raised without unnecessary material goods because the family's existence was governed by Depression-era thrift, homegrown food, flour sack dresses, and constant hard work (Cook 27). Craft-learning and mentoring relation-ships played an important role in her early education, which was befitting a female child raised before the women's movement of the 1970s. One of the first jobs she performed for her mother was to polish with milk every dusty leaf of a maze-like ivy plant until it glistened with perfection, and upon missing a single leaf, having to repolish the entire plant (Cook 27). This as-signment, designed to promote meticulousness in the young girl (a desir-able quality in a housekeeper), is typical of the other womanly arts her mother taught Richards to perfect as a child.

During high school, Richards' hard work won her trips to Washington, D.C., as a representative of Girls Nation as well as a debate scholarship to Baylor University. Yet, despite her many abilities, ambitions, and early suc-cesses, she chose the traditional path for a young woman of her time and married at the age of nineteen. Although she taught school for a few years before the first of her four children was born, Richards adapted to married life and mothering in the 1950s by exhibiting the same energy, diligence, and high standards that her mother had taught her (Cook 27). Like many women of her generation, she did not return to work until her children were grown.

Although Richards holds a degree from Baylor University and was mar-ried to a prominent and wealthy Texas attorney, she was not an upper-class woman making good on the reputation of her husband, despite her well-heeled and coiffed appearance. Even though she originally received her party's nomination for county commissioner of Travis County, her first political office, because her husband had refused to run, Richards has worked to achieve her sterling reputation and subsequent popularity as a politician in a state that doesn't cotton to women in office. Her success shouldn't be surprising, however, because Richards has never been a stranger to hard work or far from an understanding of her constituents' ex-periences.

CONCLUSION

Ann Richards became the governor of Texas partially because she uti-lized a rhetorical style that appealed to voters. In a state known for its western-style machismo, Richards needed to employ a rhetoric that transcended the non-accusatory tones of feminine style. Populism's blame-placing strategies, including the use of humor, irony, and sarcasm, allowed her to hold her own in a state that typically had not supported female politicians. Richards was able to popularize feminine style by making it stronger and more assertive and to feminize Populist style by making it less divisive and more cooperative. The fusion of feminine style with Richards' modern adaptation of a style that had deep historical roots in Texas proved to be a successful rhetorical strategy that propelled her into the nation's limelight and the governor's mansion of the state of Texas.

Chapter Six

Re-visioning and Re-framing Political Boundaries: Barbara Roberts' Response to Oregon's Budget Crisis

Molly A. Mayhead and Brenda DeVore Marshall

In November 1990, two years before "The Year of the Woman," Oregonians elected Democrat Barbara Roberts as the state's first woman governor. She won without a solid majority of the votes, barely defeating Republican David Frohnmeyer in a bitter three-way race. Simultaneously, Oregonians passed Ballot Measure 5, a property tax limitation with the potential to send the state into a catastrophic budget crisis. In this chapter we analyze Governor Roberts' response to Measure 5, the budget deficit, and the state legislature. Specifically, we argue that faced with the task of balancing a drastically reduced budget, Roberts re-visioned the boundaries of the public discourse surrounding the issue. Due to the enormity of the economic challenge, Roberts' attempt at re-visioning became sidetracked, resulting in a need for re-framing. Ultimately, Roberts did not successfully re-frame the political boundaries and did not find the voice that would bring the issues forward to the public in a meaningful way.

Roberts' response to the budget situation merits consideration on several grounds. First, few women in the United States have ever served as state governors. As communication scholars, we need more information about how women leaders solve problems, maintain credibility, persuade constituents, and govern in a traditionally male role. An examination of Governor Roberts' rhetoric, then, provides a case study of a woman in that unique position. Second, because more and more governors face huge state budget deficits and voters who are unwilling to vote themselves a tax increase to combat the money shortfall, Roberts' experience in office is becoming paradigmatic. In the 1990s, for instance, it was predicted that state revenues would fall short of spending demands, even without new programs (Lemov 22). As many as thirty-five states faced substantial deficits, and aggregate state budget reserves had fallen to an anemic 1.5 percent of expenditures (Moore 10). By examining the rhetoric of Governor Roberts, we can determine what strategies are likely to succeed or fail with the public and the legislature in responsibly addressing such politically volatile challenges.

Finally, this project will continue an interrogation of the strategies women use to address political issues as well as investigate whether women have a particular "style" and if such a style fosters rhetorical and political success. For instance, Dow and Boor Tonn have examined the "feminine style" of Ann Richards' discourse and conclude that it is different from the rhetorical strategies traditionally adopted by male political rhetors. Blankenship and Robson argue that the feminine style is "gaining legitimacy through its use by women and men in power" (353). Using Barbara Roberts as a case study, this project will confirm, reject, or extend such theories.

While establishing herself as a capable state leader was a nagging personal problem, Roberts' main challenge was Measure 5 and the state's historical reluctance for tax reform. Measure 5 capped property tax rates and shifted the burden for paying for public schools onto the state general fund. Rising costs of providing services, coupled with this new education obligation, resulted in a projected budget shortfall of $1.2 billion in the 1993–1995 biennium, and $2.5 in 1995–1997 (Hill, "Roberts" B1).

Roberts had long believed that Oregon's tax system, with high property and income taxes but no sales tax, was antiquated. Her goal, she stated, was "to do what hasn't been done before," which was to provide "true tax reform" (Hill, "Talk" A1). In order to be successful, Roberts had to persuade voters that Measure 5 would harm the state and convince them that Oregon needed a new and more rational tax system to remedy the ills of the existing tax structure as well as to combat the consequences of Measure 5.

When Roberts embarked on her revenue reform crusade, she found herself faced with a skeptical audience and bound by tough political constraints. In the first year under Measure 5, few voters saw any impact—either in promised tax relief or the gloom-and-doom forecasts of budget disaster. While the measure should have decreased property taxes, many home owners saw them rise, for it did not limit assessed values, which in many areas of the state skyrocketed due to a growing state population. "People are going to have a tough time reconciling their tax bills with the governor's plea for more money through an alternative tax," predicted political analyst Russ Dondero (Hill, "Talk" A1). "Nothing's happened yet," stated Walt Dellis, a Salem resident. "Let's see it happen," he continued. "Seeing is believing" (Hill, "Political" A18).

Governor Roberts also had to contend with the antitax mood of voters and a resistance to tax increases from an edgy legislature in an election year. "Historically," stated Dondero, "Oregonians don't like taxes. It's sort of a Pavlovian response. It may not be rational," he added, "but it's a political reality" (Hill, "Talk" A1). In fact, Oregonians have rejected sales tax measures four times. Don Arvidson, a Portland area developer, was representative of many citizens in that he believed Oregon government was too big and "has to do too much" (Hill, "Political" A18). "I'd vote for [Measure 5] again," he concluded. Bend logger Chris Brewer summed up the prevailing position when he told Roberts at a town meeting, "You must think we're pretty dumb. You're going to ask us for a sales tax. We don't want one" (Hill, "Governor" D1).

Even Democrats in the Oregon Legislature seemed wary of and reluctant to pass or even support revenue reform. The members were keenly aware of the electorate's general antipathy to taxation and their particular sensitivity to the issue after the introduction of Measure 5. Senator Bill Bradbury, for instance, viewed the public attitude as "fairly negative" and added that he doubted if anything could pass (Mapes, "Roberts Plots" E1). Democrat and House Minority Leader Peter Courtney conceded that during an election year it is "difficult for the Legislature to reach agreement on a tax plan" (Mapes, "House" B4).

In addition to this antitax, antigovernment sentiment, low credibility and approval ratings exacerbated Governor Roberts' problems. After one hundred days, the traditional time to review the merits and failures of a new government, Roberts had little success in gaining acceptance for tax reform (Mapes, "Roberts Finds" B1). Questions about her ability constantly plagued her. "There is a certain sense from my constituents," stated Baker City Democrat Mike Nelson, "that there is a lack of leadership coming from the Governor's office on Measure 5" (Mapes, "Roberts Finds" B1). "She's supposed to be leading this state," complained Delna Jones of Aloha. "I don't know what she is doing" (Mapes, "Roberts Finds" B1). The *Oregonian* described her first few months as "cautious" compared to her "outspokenness during the campaign about the state's tax structure" (Mapes, "Roberts Finds" B1). Representative Nelson concurred: "I look at how she got elected. She made hard hitting, definitive statements mapping out specific actions. Now," he added, "it appears she has retreated. She's taken a wait and see approach and it's frustrating" (Mapes, "Roberts Finds" B1).

To understand Roberts' seemingly contradictory actions, we turn to an investigation of her political rhetoric. Grounded in feminist approaches to public discourse, this inquiry draws specifically on the recent work of Sullivan and Turner as well as that of Blankenship and Robson. The ideas presented in the works of these authors inform each other and in so doing provide both a conceptual framework and a repertoire of rhetorical strategies for understanding and engaging in feminine political discourse. In the following discussion, we present an overview of the work of these scholars and extend their theoretical perspectives to forge a new understanding of Barbara Roberts' political communication as well as that of other women in elected political positions.

In *From the Margins to the Center: Contemporary Women and Political Communication*, Patricia A. Sullivan and Lynn H. Turner integrate Sandra Lipsitz Bem's discussion of gendered perceptual lenses with Joan C. Tronto's analysis of moral boundaries to provide a context for understanding feminine rhetorical strategies used in political communication. Bem argues in *The Lenses of Gender* that the culturally constructed belief systems of Western culture have created three such lenses of gender: androcentrism, gender polarization, and biological essentialism (2). Embedded in the deep structure of patriarchal cultures, androcentrism (or male-centeredness) defines male experience as the norm and female experience as "a sex-specific deviation from that norm" (2). In a familiar equation, the resulting interpretation of the norm defines man as human and woman as "other." "Put somewhat differently, [men] have used their position of public power to create cultural discourses and social institutions that automatically privilege male experience and otherize female experience" (79).

The second lens, gender polarization, uses the perceived difference between women and men as "an organizing principle for the social life of the culture" (2). That is, the perception of difference permeates the very fabric of our way of life, creating a cultural connection "between sex and virtually every other aspect of human experience" (2). According to Bem, gender polarization creates two definitional perspectives of gender. First, it "defines mutually exclusive scripts for being male and female" (80–81). Second, gender polarization defines a person who "deviates from these scripts as problematic—as unnatural or immoral from a religious perspective or as biologically anomalous or psychologically pathological from a scientific perspective" (81). This in turn creates a "gender-polarizing link between the sex of one's body and the character of one's psyche and one's sexuality" (81).

Androcentrism and gender polarization sustain each other within our culture. The perceived differences in men and women and the accompanying socialized perceptions of masculinity and femininity provide a basis for establishing the standards of normalcy, which then reinforce those differences. Consequently, deviation from those norms engenders the concepts of "other" and "other as abnormal." As Carol Tavris noted in 1992, despite women's advances in the two previous decades, "the fundamental belief in the normalcy of men, and the corresponding abnormality of women, has remained virtually untouched" (17).

The third lens, biological essentialism, "rationalizes and legitimizes" the other two lenses by "treating them as the natural and inevitable consequences of the intrinsic biological natures of women and men" (2). While acknowledging that some subtle biological differences between the sexes may exist, Bem disputes the idea that such "biological facts" have fixed meaning, arguing instead that even scientific facts are dependent on the way a "culture interprets and uses them" (3).

In the United States, the political structure resulting from these omnipresent gendered lenses defines men as insiders and women as outsiders, or other. Such systems "legitimate the voices of privileged men as political communicators and in turn dismiss the voices of women as political communicators" (Sullivan and Turner 29). How, then, do we work within or change the existing structure to allow the silenced voices to be heard?

Joan Tronto outlines one possibility as she urges scholars to rethink Western conceptions of morality that mark social orders framed by the three lenses of gender. In *Moral Boundaries: A Political Argument for an Ethic of Care,* she argues that questions and values that have traditionally informed women's lives, such as those centered on caring, have been excluded from both philosophical tradition and political theory. Such exclusion leads to a conception of the public sphere devoid of those values traditionally associated with women's world and the private sphere. For the most part, women's morality has been dismissed "as irrelevant to genuine moral argument, or as irrelevant to given political circumstances" (Tronto 4). Tronto contends that those advocating changes in the culture must avoid the pitfalls of the arguments surrounding "women's morality" and foster a more inclusive conceptualization of the values inherent in that morality. Furthermore, Tronto asserts that we must recognize that an ethic of care is not devoid of context. As she notes, "widely accepted social values constitute the context within which we interpret all moral arguments. Some ideas function as boundaries to exclude some ideas of morality from consideration" (6).

For Tronto, these Western conceptions of morality have produced three moral boundaries in which "the questions that have traditionally informed the lives of women, and servants, slaves and workers, have not informed the philosophical tradition or political theory" (3). She identifies the moral boundaries as (1) morality and politics, (2) the moral point of view, and (3) the public and private. These boundaries exist and function "to maintain the positions of the powerful" (20). As Tronto indicates, "the current boundaries of moral and political life are drawn such that the concerns and activities of the relatively powerless are omitted from the central concerns of society" (20).

In contemporary political theory, the boundary between morality and politics implies a duality that posits the two concepts as opposites with little or no possibility for interaction. This polarity leads to two stances on the relationship between morality and politics: "morality first" and "politics first" (Tronto 7). When given primacy, the perspective of morality considers moral principles as absolutes. "After moral views are fixed, right-thinking individuals should suggest to the state how political life should conform to these moral principles" (7). Building on Tronto's insight, Sullivan and Turner point out that "one manifestation of the 'morality first' boundary suggests that women lack the knowledge to serve as moral leaders in society" (35). From the "politics first" perspective, the overriding ethic is the Machiavellian principle that "the end justifies the means." Gaining and preserving power are the principal goals. "In this view, moral values should only be introduced into politics in accordance with the requirements of these political concerns" (7).

The moral point of view boundary suggests that moral decisions should and can be grounded in reason, objectivity, distance, and disinterest. Thus, the significance of emotion and the contextual issues of social and political circumstances in daily life are denied. Morality becomes associated only with universal reason and only with the conceptual nature of moral thought. Individual circumstances and actors are of little concern in reaching a conclusion or choosing an action. In practice, this moral boundary excludes women and their experiences.

The third boundary described by Tronto, that between public and private life, in large part maintains the other boundaries. Feminists identify this division between public and private life as one of the major cultural constraints women face, for it restricts women to the private realm and thereby silences them. As we know, one of the greatest challenges facing women reformers of the nineteenth century was gaining access to the speaker's platform. "The issue was not speaking as such, but speaking to males, speaking on an equal basis with males, speaking that challenged male authority and rationality" (Campbell and Jerry 124). As Karlyn Kohrs Campbell and Claire Jerry note, "women were attacked for their moral reform efforts because rhetorical action is, as defined by gender roles, a masculine domain" (125). Within this cultural context, society views women as lacking the capacity for reason and therefore as intellectually inferior to men. Additionally, women represent sentiment and therefore are morally superior to men (Sullivan and Turner 45). Thus, the demarcation between public and private life constructs the notion of woman as "incapable of autonomous and detached decision-making" (Sullivan and Turner 45) and, consequently, unsuited for public and political life.

While noting that these three boundaries "block the effectiveness of women's morality arguments" and thus their full participation in public life, Tronto does not call for their abolition (10–11). She argues that such action would "jeopardize the very basis of modern political life and the possibilities for feminism and for freedom" (10). Rather, she calls for a redrawing of the boundaries to foster women's access to public and political life.

As indicated previously, Sullivan and Turner draw on Bem and Tronto to explain the ways in which some women have moved from the margins of political life to its center. To function effectively within the patriarchal structure created by these moral boundaries and maintained by gendered lenses, Sullivan and Turner describe how women working within the world of contemporary politics find new ways to make their voices heard by adopting one of three rhetorical strategies: denying, confronting and accommodating, or re-visioning (46).

Those women who adopt the strategy of denying refuse or fail to recognize the barriers they face in the traditional male world of politics. They enter this realm with faith in a rationalist paradigm that suggests that "the rules for political communication are clear and success will follow if those rules are followed" (Sullivan and Turner 46). This belief allows them to deny the existence of moral boundaries or to view them as permeable. In a study of the rhetoric of Lani Guinier, President Clinton's nominee for Assistant Attorney General for Civil Rights, Sullivan and Turner argue that Guinier failed to recognize the existence of boundaries that would create obstacles for her. Throughout the nomination process, Guinier continued to believe in the democratic system—in the "ideals of rights, individualism, equality, and fairness" (65). Guinier's denial of the operative political boundaries and their entrenched status in the establishment left her open to attack from each of the moral boundaries identified by Tronto.

Unlike the deniers, those women in politics who confront and accommodate the boundaries "recognize barriers to their participation as leaders in political processes and communicate as though they will be able to circumvent those barriers" (Sullivan and Turner 47). These women recognize they are disadvantaged in the world of politics but do not view themselves as disempowered in that context. They know the playing field is not level and understand the gamelike nature of politics. They believe they will be successful if they discover the "appropriate tactics" to respond to each situation they face (Sullivan and Turner 48). In other words, women operating from this position believe the world is rational and that if they operate rationally, they too can be successful players in the political game. Their preferred method of operation lies in a strategy of confronting and accommodating; that is, "the three moral boundaries, all three grounded in reason, may be finessed if the speaker simply strikes the appropriate balance between confronting and accommodating" (Sullivan and Turner 48). Even women who successfully negotiate this balance between confronting and accommodating face additional obstacles, however: "When women rely upon this strategy, they overlook the power of double binds—the irrational 'catch 22'—that they will be criticized regardless of their choices as communicators" (48). Using a telling metaphor to describe the contemporary political double bind that women face, Jamieson contends that "women who succeed in politics and public life will be scrutinized under a different lens from that applied to successful men" (*Beyond* 16).

Sullivan and Turner provide a detailed analysis of the rhetoric of Hillary Rodham Clinton to illustrate the inherent trap within the confrontation-and-accommodation strategy. Specifically, they focus on the discourse surrounding Rodham Clinton's role as chair of the president's task force on America's health care system. In her public discourse surrounding this issue, Rodham Clinton did not challenge the concept of established boundaries. Rather, she adopted a classic confrontation and accommodation approach. "Her rhetorical style suggests a belief in women's abilities to study situations, figure out where the boundaries are, and then educate themselves to surmount them" (69). Sullivan and Turner conclude that Rodham Clinton confronted the moral boundaries "only in the most obvious sense" and that rather than redraw the moral boundaries, she accommodated them (82).

Women who engage in re-visioning adopt a perspective distinct from those who deny the existence of boundaries as well as those who recognize them but maneuver within them through confrontation and accommodation. Re-visioners recognize the existence of the boundaries but are unwilling to work within the established paradigm because they disagree with the value system that grounds it. Like Tronto, re-visioners concede the need for boundaries in order to maintain a viable political system but believe the existing moral and political boundaries need to be redrawn. Re-visioners believe that "naming in politics has been a male prerogative" and that new ways of seeing the world need to be valued (49). "When the boundaries are 'redrawn' and moral decision-making is re-visioned, political decision-making will take into account the value orientations of 'others' (i.e., women, slaves, people of color) who have been on the margins of discourse" (49).

For explication of the re-visioning strategy, Sullivan and Turner focus on the rhetoric of U.S. Attorney General Janet Reno, giving special attention to her discourse surrounding events at the Branch Davidian complex in Waco. During this time "Reno emerged as a powerful and forthright speaker, a public figure who was willing to take responsibility for her actions" (96) by speaking from "a morality grounded in 'care' rather than a morality grounded in 'rights' " (98). Thus, "Reno's discourse offers possibilities for re-visioning moral boundaries and looking *at* rather than *through* the lenses of gender" (110).

While we agree with Sullivan and Turner's philosophical standpoint, it is our contention that the feminine stances of denying, confronting and accommodating, and re-visioning are not rhetorical strategies but rather conceptual constructs or paradigms that are operationalized through the application of more specific strategies of public discourse. Moreover, although the ideological categories described by Sullivan and Turner may provide sufficient contextual frames for the analysis of feminine political rhetoric outside electoral politics, as in the cases of Lani Guinier, Hillary Rodham Clinton, and Janet Reno, we argue that women holding elected political office face additional contradictions, double binds, and other unforeseen obstacles not encountered by those in the non-electoral public arena. Therefore, an additional rhetorical paradigm must be employed to better describe the discourse strategies women in elected office use to navigate the boundaries of contemporary electoral politics.

Women elected to political office, like those working in other public sector arenas, do indeed operate from each of the conceptual paradigms described by Sullivan and Turner. Furthermore, women candidates and elected officials in increasing numbers adopt a re-visioning stance, which recognizes boundaries even as it encourages a redrawing or redefining of them. Certainly, those embracing an ideological political stance employ such tactics and often find that nothing short of abolition of the boundaries allows one to function outside of them. As noted previously, Tronto wisely urges us to re-vision and consequently redraw rather than abolish the boundaries that provide a necessary mechanism for making sense of our world. Moreover, re-visioning on its own has proved to be of limited applicability across a range of political contexts. This limitation manifests itself in total or partial failure within the re-visioned boundary. Working through re-visioning, a woman politician respects the existence of the boundaries while confronting the necessity of redrawing them to provide a more inclusive and caring perspective in which to ground her political goals. However, the existing political system and the perceptions of those she represents often do not allow this to happen. While voters may decry the status quo, they also have little faith in unproven changes to the existing system. This doubt is compounded when the challenges themselves seem to have little resemblance to the way things have been done before and when they come from someone perceived as a foreigner in the political realm. What choices does the woman politician have when she finds herself in this untenable position?

At such points, women candidates and officeholders must find another perspective from which to function. We contend that an additional rhetorical paradigm, re-framing, comes into existence at such times. As the female politician begins to assess the success or failure of her re-visioning perspective, she begins to re-vision the re-visioning by re-framing it. Re-framing entails a morphing of the lines between the established boundaries described by Tronto and the newly drawn boundaries created through re-visioning. Such a perspective allows one to move back and forth, as the situation dictates, between the existing boundaries and those one wishes to establish. Ultimately, re-framing moves beyond the re-visioned boundary to achieve a more inclusive and synergistic perspective that allows the female officeholder to overcome many of the obstacles inherent in the other constructs available to her.

In order to operationalize these rhetorical paradigms, especially re-visioning and re-framing, women politicians adopt specific discourse tactics that showcase their authentic voices. These strategies emerge from the characteristics of feminine style found in political rhetoric. To describe these characteristics, we turn to the work of Jane Blankenship and Deborah C. Robson.

These scholars examine feminine style in political rhetoric through the discourse of congresswomen in campaign and governance contexts. In "A 'Feminine Style' in Women's Political Discourse: An Exploratory Essay," Blankenship and Robson argue that a feminine style does exist and is adopted by both men and women in their political rhetoric. The authors identify five characteristics common to the feminine style of political discourse: basing political judgments on concrete, lived experience; valuing inclusivity and the relational nature of being; conceptualizing the power of public office as a capacity to "get things done" and empower others; approaching policy formation holistically; and moving women's issues to the forefront of the public arena (359). These characteristics recall the earlier work of Campbell, as well as that of Dow and Boor Tonn, and are compatible with the notion of moral and political boundaries developed by Tronto and Sullivan and Turner.

Given our understanding of the constructs from which female politicians may operate and the strategies they may adopt to accomplish their goals, we turn to an example of the ways in which these two concepts function together in the rhetorical strategies Governor Roberts adopted to respond to the political situation she faced upon election. In response to the pending budget crisis described earlier in this chapter, Governor Roberts launched her program "The Conversation with Oregon." She designed this plan to include voters in discussions about revenue replacement. Specifically, Roberts conceived the conversation to gather voter opinions and to engage them in planning for the state's future. A press release from her office elaborates her justification:

Traditionally, politicians would turn to polls and advertising to push a tax reform plan. But neither of those shopworn approaches would have helped Oregon work through its budget troubles and find a solution that works. That's why we designed the Conversation. We are giving people the information and the power to help us answer the most critical question Oregon faces: What kind of future do we want for our state? What level of public services do we want and need? And finally, how are we going to provide for those services? ("Press Release" n.p)

The conversations took place in Town Hall–style meetings led by trained volunteers. Participants answered questions regarding their perceptions of government spending, government efficiency, the desirability of state services, and specifically about the ramifications of Measure 5. Approximately 900 meetings were scheduled and 10,000 individuals participated. The events revealed that most voters did not know how government or budgets operate, most believed that government could be run more efficiently, and most did not want a sales tax to replace revenue lost under the measure. Roberts summarized her findings in a December 12, 1991 press release: "I talked with about 10,000 Oregonians and I listened to them. They learned more about how state government works, and I learned about what they expect from government. They have sent a clear message," she concluded. "We in government must do our job better. That will be the starting point for my efforts" (qtd. in Weeks 61).

Roberts' initiation of the conversation demonstrated that she attempted both to redraw and re-vision the political and moral boundaries. By their very nature, the conversations valued inclusivity, for they theoretically gave a "voice" to those who had been marginalized in the past. The governor believed that once Oregonians knew what was at stake for the state, they would work with her to create a new Oregon. As she stated in the Tom McCall Lecture Series:

I believe my job is clear. My job is to build bridges between those who demand property tax relief and those who demand quality schools. My job is to build partnerships between those who have and those who have not. My job is to tell Oregonians about my dreams for Oregon's future, and to trust in my belief that—given the facts—Oregonians will choose health over hurt, caring over catastrophe. ("Tom McCall" 14)

Roberts' statement reflects a desire to abandon the business-as-usual approach of government. Rather than focusing simply on cut-and-dried facts and policies, Roberts attempted to redefine how state government should operate. Unlike the typical politician concerned with placating colleagues and special interest groups, she envisioned government as a cooperative effort between citizens and the elected body. Thus, she attempted to work outside the traditional political system by re-visioning that system. Roberts conceptualized the power of her public office as a way to empower others; that is, to bring citizens together to get things done and envision what was right for the state. Governor Roberts never shied away from revealing her own vision for the state, however. At times she almost waxed poetic as she wove threads of philosophy with pragmatic issues into a tapestry for the future. In a speech to the Oregon Employment and Training Conference, for instance, she stated:

Imagine . . .

An Oregon where not a single mind is wasted;

An ever diversified economy;

An Oregon where the economy and the environment exist hand in hand;

An Oregon where health care, housing, and healthy wages are available to every Oregonian;

A State government where planning, management, and thrift share equal billing with compassion, respect and commitment—the best of business, the best of family.

A State government that is lean but not mean. ("Oregon" n.p.)

Working both inside and outside traditional boundaries proved tricky for Roberts, however. At times she felt that her conversations were not having an impact. In her May 18, 1991, speech to the League of Women Voters, for instance, Roberts acknowledged that "this process of reaching a solution makes some folks very uneasy. They keep asking where the leadership is. They want a plan, they want to send something to the ballot, they want bells and whistles—and they don't believe that I'm producing that" (15). This assessment of the situation proved quite telling, for it indicates a gap between what citizens wanted—traditional politics and approaches—and what they got from Governor Roberts. An inkling of the inadequacy of her re-visioning construct thus surfaced. The Conversation wasn't selling, despite her belief that it was, as she stated in an interview with the *Oregonian*, "a good educational tool" (Mapes, "Roberts Rejects" B4). "This is a real process," Roberts contended. "It is really intended to involve [the voters]" (Hill, "Talk" A1).

The press and legislators were not kind in their evaluations of Roberts' efforts. Wayne Thompson, in an editorial titled "Salem Dodgeball," argued that "Roberts does recognize the disaster that lies ahead for state agencies once Measure 5 builds up to its head of steam in the mid-1990s. But to deal with it she proposes little more than a statewide public relations effort" (B6). Part of the problem with an approach like the Conversation with Oregon stemmed from the fact that no one could predict the results. And yet, in order to craft a tax plan, the data had to be hard, concrete, and specific.

Interpreting the citizen responses proved difficult and, in actuality, undermined the governor's own policy goals. House Democratic Leader Peter Courtney had a number of misgivings. He believed that taking the Conversation to voters would "create expectations that can't be met" (Hill, "Talk" A1). He later predicted that Roberts would not have enough support for a new tax plan. "I don't think the consensus is going to be strong enough . . . to get the sufficient number of votes in both houses" (Mapes, "House" B4). Part of the problem, Courtney concluded, was that Oregonians were unsure or unconvinced of the serious impact of Measure 5 cuts.

While Roberts may have redrawn and re-visioned boundaries, her message for Oregon did not seem to resonate with the voters or legislators. The governor's attempt at working outside the system angered legislators and made it difficult for her to get tax reform accomplished. Realizing that the Conversation with Oregon was not building consensus for a new tax plan, she began to re-frame her vision. In June 1992, Roberts announced that she planned to call a special session for legislators to consider a tax plan she wanted sent to the voting public in September. Roberts did not seek legislative assistance in crafting her plan, and in fact her strategy "seemed to bypass the Legislature as much as possible, to tell legislators they can campaign against the proposal, but that Oregonians ought to have a right to vote on the plan" (Mapes, "Roberts Plots" E1). This strategy led one representative to comment that Roberts was taking a "fairly arrogant approach" to accomplish her goals (Mapes, "Governor's" A1).

In addition to resenting their lack of participation in designing the tax plan, legislators opposed the governor's chosen release date for it. September was just too soon, many claimed. Lawmakers wanted instead to release the plan to the voters in November. Representative Courtney, for one, was " 'very down' about the prospects for a successful ballot measure" (Mapes, "Roberts Plots" E1). He did not believe that there was enough time to examine the plan for flaws or to build support for it among constituents (Mapes,

"Roberts Plots" E1). Courtney's fears were realized: On July 1, 1992, the Legislature voted to reject Governor Roberts' tax plan.

Emotions ran high and nerves were raw after the plan's defeat. "It was the failure of the Legislature," Governor Roberts told the media at her press conference. "I've given this my best effort" (McCarthy, A14). Two days after the plan went down, the governor's Chief of Staff, Patricia McCaig, told the *Oregonian* that the Legislature had shown disrespect for Roberts because she was a woman. Three days later, Roberts herself told the Associated Press that there was a different expectation of her than there would have been of a male governor (Mapes, "Roberts Not Graceful" C3). But, she later downplayed the issue of gender, saying it was a "minor factor, perhaps" (Mapes, "Roberts Not Graceful" C3).

Clearly, Roberts attempted to work outside the system. She was unwilling to compromise on the content or release date of her tax package. That failure, combined with the less-than-expected response from voters, ultimately doomed Roberts to defeat. She subsequently agreed to support a tax plan designed by the legislature—if it wasn't a band-aid approach to revenue shortfall: "Anything that moves us toward a solution, I'm in favor of," she said (Hill, "State" A1).

While the Conversation with Oregon allowed Governor Roberts to re-vision the political boundaries, the citizens and legislature did not accept her vision for Oregon. Roberts believed that shared government would be a way to solve the state's woes. Once the citizens and legislators rejected her vision, she appropriately moved to re-frame the boundaries of that vision. However, in doing so she committed some tactical errors in terms of the rhetorical strategies she embraced.

Most significantly, Roberts' re-framing of the situation proved faulty. By attempting to craft a tax plan without legislative input, she played a game of political chicken. Rather than build on the innovation of the Conversation with Oregon, she simply confronted the legislature in a dogmatic and unstrategic manner. Quite simply, the legislature did not blink. This was a dire miscalculation on her part. Politics-as-usual, after months of waiting for the results of the Conversation, rang hollow, and more importantly, had little chance for success.

Roberts had returned to the legislative battleground armed with the belief that the Conversation with Oregon provided her with needed ammunition to accomplish her goals. While she stopped to reassess the climate for tax reform, she failed to recognize her responsiblity to help create a shared vision for the state. For instance, she did not at any time argue the need for or importance of state services. Rather than justify and defend the job that state government does, Roberts simply announced in her 1992 State of the State

Address that she was making numerous reductions in state agencies and organizations: "I will cut 4,000 jobs from state government in this budget period, and I will start immediately. . . . I will eliminate roughly 2,000 more jobs, most of necessity, from our largest budgets, human resources, education, and public safety" (6). She also admitted that the "role your government plays has changed" (2). By not standing up for government and government services, Roberts essentially undermined her re-visioning and re-framing of the political system based on a notion of shared community. She eventually yielded to the perception that citizens simply cared about themselves and decreasing their tax bills. And, her proposed cuts made it look like she agreed that the state of Oregon had been wasting the taxpayers' money.

As noted at the beginning of this discussion, scholars have identified specific strategies that women politicians adopt when navigating political boundaries. Barbara Roberts' experience with Oregon's budget crisis, however, instructs us that a modification of those precepts is warranted. In initiating the Conversation with Oregon, she re-visioned and then re-framed the political boundaries in her attempt to include citizen participation in the budgeting process. In its ideal and purest form, this re-visioning and re-framing allow the rhetor to overcome the politics-as-usual obstacles encountered in confronting and accommodating. Unfortunately for Roberts, her attempt at re-framing was marred by the tactical errors mentioned previously.

Re-visioning and re-framing to achieve the inclusivity Roberts desired can work only if certain criteria are met. First, the vision presented must be specifically detailed. While Roberts told the public that she was ultimately cutting 6,000 state jobs, she never predicted the impact those cuts would have on voters. How would their tax situation be improved, for instance, with a more "streamlined" state government? Conversely, would fewer state workers mean longer waiting periods for state services? No one in her administration really knew or had investigated the answers to these questions, causing a skepticism about Roberts and her plan that few could reconcile.

So, if a rhetor decides to re-vision and subsequently re-frame boundaries, she still must deal with the traditional need to ground her efforts in a carefully articulated and detailed vision. Furthermore, inclusivity works only if the vision being constructed is truly shared. As Roberts offered in her 1992 State of the State Address, "we will not satisfy Oregon's needs and we will not realize Oregon's great promise unless we all face our challenges and opportunities together" (8). In a quick burst of honesty, she admitted that Oregon must "restructure" its tax system, which meant a sales tax, to achieve the vision. Unfortunately for Roberts, Oregonians simply did not want a sales tax. So, while Roberts and the citizens may have shared a partial vision of a better Oregon, the varied notions of what was needed to realize it did not mesh. As our analysis of Roberts' rhetoric suggests, politically viable re-visioning and re-framing that enable successful navigation of the political boundaries require appropriate discourse strategies that offer a rhetor's audience a unified view of reality.

Chapter Seven

Christine Todd Whitman and the Ideology of the New Jersey Governorship

Kristina Horn Sheeler

In 1993 Christine Todd Whitman was elected as the first woman governor of New Jersey, one of the most powerful governorships in the country, by virtue of the state's constitution. As an influential tax-cutting Republican, Whitman is praised as a vital part of the ongoing so-called Republican Revolution, bringing power back to the states and the people in the mid-1990s. As Peter Jennings stated before Whitman's Republican Response to President Clinton's State of the Union Address in January 1995, she "is one of the fastest rising stars in the Republican party . . . a tax cutting Republican on the move" ("Introduction"). She was seriously considered as a possible running mate for Bob Dole in 1996, and already excitement is mounting regarding a possible vice-presidential bid from Republican front-runner George W. Bush.

Whitman's election and subsequent notoriety are significant within the realm of American liberal political discourse, juxtaposing two terms that have a problematic history when considered concurrently: gender and leadership. The purpose of this chapter is to assess the ideological implications of political leadership as defined by Christine Todd Whitman in New Jersey, considering whether and how she reinforces the existing ideology and/or negotiates a productive space where women as well as men have more political latitude. After discussing the gendered implications of liberal democracy as it has been performed in New Jersey, I will focus on the first and second inaugurals as well as the radio addresses of Christine Todd Whitman in order to demonstrate how she articulates liberal democracy in New Jersey.

I begin by discussing our liberal democratic political culture and its related practices, arguing that masculine expectations have been reinscribed
as the norm. This is no different for the political practices that have been articulated in New Jersey. Thus, in order to enact power, Christine Todd Whitman must negotiate masculine political expectations. Next, I argue that
Whitman puts her version of New Jersey ideology into motion by using
New Jersey statehood ideographically to create a "people" united as a family. Whitman creates this collectively defined citizenry by negotiating the
norms of masculine control required by her office along with feminine
norms of inclusion and diversity, suggesting that New Jersey will be "reinvented" with her leadership. In particular, Whitman relies on the metaphor
of the family to "reinvent" New Jersey not as an impersonal bureaucracy but
as a site where government and its citizens may work together, focusing on
the visibility of citizens as leaders in a person-oriented family. Ultimately,
the type of family that Whitman creates defines the relationship of citizens
with and the presence of citizens within state government. However, while
Whitman may enact an ideology that appears to move New Jersey forward,
the question is whether she offers true structural change.

GENDER AND THE IDEOLOGY OF LIBERAL DEMOCRACY

Ever since this country's founding, our liberal democratic political culture has demanded a particular type of person to fulfill positions of leadership. As these expectations have been practiced historically, they have
developed in such a way as to go unquestioned (Duerst-Lahti and Kelly
21–22; Brown, *Manhood* 1–4). The result is a political ideology taken for
granted as objective rather than as constructed, and the invisibility of these
expectations only serves to increase their viability. Catherine MacKinnon
explains that the norm of objectivity "legitimates itself by reflecting its view
of society, a society it helps make by so seeing it, and calling that view, and
that relation, rationality. . . . What counts as reason is that which corre-
sponds to the way things are" (162). Marx would explain this phenomenon
as thought that denies its social determination so as to become naturalized
and dehistoricized; thought that has somehow become separated or "un-
stuck" from the material conditions of its production (Eagleton 79, 89).

Furthermore, such an ideology is gendered in that it motivates masculine
entailments privileging strength, aggression, self-interest, ordered activity,
and independence as leadership norms while marginalizing cooperation,
consensus-building, deference, and selfless decision making (Brown,
States 152–164). Sue Tolleson-Rinehart and Jeanie Stanley go so far as to

argue that "the epistemology and even the ontology of leadership . . . have been inextricably associated with masculinity" (2). When women public officials attempt to negotiate the prevailing political (masculine) ideology, they are more likely found inadequate since they are more easily identified with societal constructions of femininity and are considered symbolic, a token, unusual (Tolleson-Rinehart and Stanley 2). "Those who are masculine or who perform masculinity well have advantages in gaining and holding leadership positions in governance situations" (Duerst-Lahti and Kelly 19). The result is to reify rather than question the underlying gender constructions of political practice.

Christine Todd Whitman operates within an ideological structure of liberal democracy. According to Michael McGee, ideology manifests itself in political language made up of sloganlike terms that guide behavior in the particular political culture ("Ideograph" 5). The way the democratic imagination has been formed to conceive of political participation and leadership is limited in its purview, relying on a political language that casts aside rhetoric for rationality, discards passionate appeals for detachment, rejects diversity for homogeneity, and upholds the Framers' ideal, from which deliberation has degenerated. The resulting impulse is to discipline and contain democratic practice within narrow limits dictated by liberal political ideology. After all, democratic deliberation that is not contained becomes a battlefield instilling "fear of the mob" (T. Smith 15), allowing rhetorical strategizing and advocacy to pass for deliberative engagement. Ironically, however, in the name of democracy, American controlling impulses are justified, undermining the very practices that democratic political culture believes itself to be perpetuating. The rhetorical implications of these moves are significant, indeed, as they set up a feminine-versus-masculine binary pair: images of chaos, passion, irrationality, and "body out of control" justify the cleansing, ordering/homogenizing, excluding, and masculine-rational tendencies required to keep democracy in check. As Robert Ivie explains, it is this very attitude toward democracy that "motivates us to defeat . . . diversity as a threat to national security rather than to engage differences rhetorically as a fact of democratic life" (491).

Furthermore, McGee argues that the ideograph is the "link between rhetoric and ideology" ("Ideograph" 1). He explains that ideology is present in the language used to communicate it, in the public motives it calls forth (4). "Ideology in practice is a political language, preserved in rhetorical documents, with the capacity to dictate decision and control public belief and behavior" (5). Analyzing ideographs indicates structures of public motives, which "control 'power' and . . . influence . . . each individual's 'reality' " (5). As a result, humans are "conditioned" to a vocabulary that provides guides for belief and behavior and functions as a rhetoric of control. This vocabulary is full of nuances of meaning that each individual will understand and follow without question. Ideographs act "as agents of political consciousness" (7).

McGee identifies liberty, freedom, and equality as important and powerful ideographs in American culture. While these usages also may be found in the public discourse of other women governors, what is most prominent in Whitman's discourse is the discussion and definition of New Jersey statehood, especially as it helps to define a concrete history and future of the state. As McGee explains, what is important is not the content that ideographs identify but their "concrete history as usages" ("Ideograph" 10). Ideographs have a diachronic dimension, encompassing the way the term has evolved over time, and a synchronic dimension, speaking to the way the ideographs relate to one another in a specific moment in time.

The challenge for Whitman is that liberal democracy as it is currently sutured justifies patriarchal control over feminine inclusion and gender diversity. As a result, such women leaders as Whitman often find themselves in a "double bind," a rhetorical construction that has only two alternatives: one that limits their power and one that undermines their exercise of power should they ever break through the constraints placed upon them (Jamieson, *Beyond* 13–14). One of these "double binds" Jamieson labels "femininity/competence" (*Beyond* 120–145). Even though Jamieson does not articulate a way out of the problem, she provides evidence that women are competent leaders who have found a variety of ways to negotiate the double bind. Furthermore, her evidence ruptures the prevailing masculine political ideology, underscoring its incomplete suturing as a site of struggle. As Jamieson explains, "[w]e are getting to know tough and caring female senators and congresspersons, cabinet secretaries and first spouses, anchors and reporters, and justices of the Supreme Court. And they no longer enter our world, in Ruth Bader Ginsburg's phrase, as 'tokens of one' " (145). Christine Todd Whitman provides further evidence of this contradiction.

GUBERNATORIAL DISCOURSE

In her inaugural speeches, Christine Todd Whitman begins her formal exercise of governmental power, bringing together a whole host of cultural, political, and ideological practices. Her inaugurals are ritual practices dictated by the political system while they simultaneously direct government control; thus, they are a performance of ideology. Yet, these performances are not uncritical. An ideology does not reproduce itself naturally but is transformed through hegemonic practice as a society enacts, accommodates, contests, and puts language and meaning into practice. The key element of this process is the "constitution of the subject, where the subject is precisely he or she who simultaneously speaks and initiates action in discourse . . . and in the world" (Charland 133). Hegemonic practices provide the potential for change, as Whitman acts within and responds to the people and leadership culture. Furthermore, Whitman calls her supporters into being as subjects through the use of a political vocabulary that creates meaning and legitimizes her use of power. Subject positions are not fixed, however, but once they become accepted can serve to limit choices. Charland finds this a kind of constrained freedom where subjects must re-articulate the narrative within the language structure to incorporate a sense of agency, and in so doing make various attempts at identification (137–141).

In her inaugurals, Whitman not only chooses the direction for her term in office but also re-articulates the terms of the story she is writing in order to craft a sense of agency within strongly articulated ideological expectations. This becomes clearer upon discussion of the ideograph of New Jersey statehood, the construction of "the people," and the time-space-structure of the first and second inaugurals. Furthermore, Whitman's radio addresses, begun in her second term in office, provide further elaboration of her second inaugural and carry out in concrete form her ideological choices.

New Jersey as Ideograph

One of the rhetorical features of Whitman's inaugurals is her use of "New Jersey" ideographically to construct a leadership position and unite various voices within the state. "New Jersey" becomes a container of references both historical and present, extending from notions of statehood to include current configurations of Whitman's "New Jersey family." New Jersey, first and foremost as the name of a state formed with this country's founding, is infused with a variety of historically constructed expectations. Just as liberal democracy has masculine expectations, the notion of statehood is similarly masculine, carrying with it a political vocabulary that motivates public belief and actions. Wendy Brown argues that "not merely the structure and discourse but the ethos of the liberal state appears to be socially masculine; its discursive currencies are rights rather than needs, individuals rather than relations, autogenesis rather than interdependence, interests rather than shared circumstances" (*States* 184). MacKinnon, citing numerous feminist scholars, goes even further, arguing that "the state is male" and as a result "coercively and authoritatively constitutes the social order in the interest of men as a gender—through its legitimating norms, forms, relation to society, and substantive policies" (161–162).

Such a masculine bias plays out in the discourse on statehood by privileging objectivity and rationality as decision-making norms while it legitimates the status quo and reinforces power dynamics that "most closely adhere to its own ideal of fairness" (MacKinnon 163). As MacKinnon discusses several specific cases, she comes to the conclusion that the discourse on statehood as enacted in the constitution and laws of the state "demean all women ideologically" (165). What she uncovers is that state policy becomes equated with masculine norms and, by extension, that statehood carries with it a rhetoric of control that reinscribes gender relations along traditional and hierarchical lines.

Such is the case as New Jersey statehood has developed over time—diachronically. The New Jersey governor is among the most powerful throughout the country by virtue of the state's redesigned constitution of 1947 (Salmore and Salmore 128). Additionally, there is no lieutenant governor, elected secretary of state, treasurer, or attorney general. Clearly, the governor must be an independent and directive individual.

The modern New Jersey governorship claims many advantages for the governor when it comes to agenda setting and policy decisions. "Broad veto powers, domination of the budget process, use of executive orders, wide-ranging appointment powers, the likelihood of reelection, and the absence of a legislative veto constitute a formidable armaterium for the chief executive" (Salmore and Salmore 131). Most New Jersey governors have few problems carrying out their policy objectives. However, that does not mean that the modern governor has an easy time swaying public opinion. The broad powers of the governor require dealing with an ever more assertive legislature as well as a "small elite—in politics, the media, and the business community" (Salmore and Salmore 135). Furthermore, there is no New Jersey—oriented commercial television station, and no statewide newspaper. Thus, the New Jersey governor has a challenging job when it comes to unifying public opinion in support of policy issues and activating that public to influence the legislature.

Whitman uses "New Jersey" ideographically by juxtaposing traditional norms of masculine control with feminine inclusion and diversity, which work themselves out through her metaphor of the family, most clearly declared through her first inaugural theme of "New Jersey, One Family" and extended to the second inaugural focus on "Many Faces, One Family." She puts her ideology into place through this political vocabulary, using it to motivate and unify the citizens of her state while apparently mindful of the diachronic nature of the ideograph as it has been defined before her.

Diachronically, the ideograph of New Jersey statehood is associated with strength, power, control, and tradition—masculine virtues in our liberal democracy. Christine Todd Whitman negotiates and redefines the ideology of statehood. In her first inaugural address of January 1994, Whitman enacts her stance as a decision maker and tax cutter and defines her vision of state democracy as one that "must be 'of' and 'by the people' " (2). She states that "Government must trust and listen to the people, or it is not a democracy" (2). The state decision-making apparatus must be "open" and decisions "based on consensus," concepts which require a "fundamental change" in the very workings of New Jersey government (3). After all, Whitman is "not one of the boys" and things are "going to be different" around the state as she embarks on the next four years of "reinventing" state government (3).

New Jersey state government may be "reinvented" under Whitman's term in office from a powerful autonomous entity to one that is open, collaborative, and listens to the people. However, that reinvention takes the shape of reinventing government institutions, "the foundations of our democracy" ("Inaugural" 2), rather than giving the public more decision-making capacity within civil society. As Whitman outlines her plans for strengthening the state of New Jersey, she likens the state to a "powerful engine of prosperity" (4), of corporations, institutions, and a competitive business that must not lose out to other states. The state must be "efficient [and] cost-effective" (7), control the education of its children, protect its citizens from crime, and be demanding and tough. New Jersey is a business that is efficient, strong, and demands high standards from its school children. New Jersey remains structured from the top down.

In her second inaugural, delivered at the new Performing Arts Center in Newark, she asserts: "I have made it a hallmark of my administration to part from tradition" ("Remarks" 1). She proclaims that "the arts are an integral part of any civilized society and every proud state" (1). Whitman is "filled with hope for New Jersey" that it will continue to employ its workers, stand tough against criminals, standardize its children's education, protect the environment, and thrive economically. New Jersey is a place where the momentum is working for the future of New Jersey's people, who remain in a dependent relationship with the state. While this clearly resonates with the ideograph of New Jersey statehood diachronically, it is also a contradiction to Whitman's more inclusive open-government ideal. The people are not involved in the decision-making process, but are taken care of. The people are not trusted, but are educated in a "standardized" manner. In fact, the people are constructed as absent from the democratic workings of the state.

McGee explains that ideographs have a history of usage that gets in the way of "pure thought," making it difficult to think about the ideas apart from their history, defined by the material conditions of the society in which we live ("Ideograph" 9). Perhaps this is the case not only for the public, but for their leaders as well. New Jersey statehood is an ideograph full of masculine entailments, making it difficult for Whitman to put into practice an open, consensus-oriented, citizen-inclusive state government. McGee cautions that the power of ideographs is not in their content but in their usage. It is not enough to talk about open government; the proof is in the way the ideograph of New Jersey statehood is used. Whitman pairs statehood with a traditionally feminine-oriented concern, the family, in her first inaugural theme in order to enact and reinvent that statehood from her point of view. Through "New Jersey, One Family" as well as her second inaugural theme, "Many Faces, One Family," Whitman has the potential to illustrate how ideology functions as a dynamic force both diachronically and synchronically, with the power to appear consonant, "but not always the *same* consonance and unity" (McGee, "Ideograph" 14). By considering how the family metaphor is used in relation to statehood, we may ask whether Whitman begins to open a productive space for herself and all people in a governorship attune to gender relations.

Whitman attempts to redefine New Jersey as a family in her first inaugural and carries this through her second inaugural and her radio addresses. In both her inaugurals, her own family is present, and she refers to each member by name and thanks each one: "I especially want to thank my husband John and my two children, Kate and Taylor, for standing by me during a long tough campaign" ("Inaugural" 1). And similarly in 1998: "I want to thank my family: my parents, who gave me life and love; my sister Kate and brother Dan, on whom I count for inspiration and advice; my children, Kate and Taylor, who have taught me so much and make me so proud; and my husband, John, who has given me love, patience, and comfort throughout our years together" ("Remarks" 1).

What becomes significant is not that she thanks her family and they are present, for many politicians follow such a norm at their inaugural. What is significant is that her family, visually present, is being used strategically to put her ideology into practice. By bringing traditionally private sphere issues into the state realm, Whitman begins to assert her power over them. Louis Althusser argues that in order for the state to maintain power, it must control "distinct and specialized institutions" that function privately, such as the family, the Church, and (in some cases) the school (Althusser 110–111, 117).

Visually and verbally, Whitman has brought the family, a traditionally private sphere concern, into the public realm of her governorship, making it easier to extend the metaphor to the state level as *the* New Jersey family. When talking about family, she talks about "our family." When discussing children, she proclaims "our children." Throughout her inaugurals, she uses inclusive pronouns *we* and *us*, emphasizing "I can't do it alone. I need your help, your wisdom and your support" ("Inaugural" 2). As she outlines her legislative agenda for her first term, she discusses the impact on families that "have car payments and credit card bills" ("Inaugural" 4). And, she concludes by expressing her hope for this inclusive vision of "one family, one community, one state" and emphasizes how all New Jerseyans are connected, just like a family: "When one of us is out of work, homeless, cannot read, or is a victim of violent crime, we all suffer. And when we help one another succeed, we all succeed" ("Inaugural" 9–10). By extending the family metaphor to the state realm, Whitman defines strategically her vision of governmental control and puts into play masculine and feminine expectations, dynamically negotiating the ideology of the New Jersey governorship.

Her second inaugural continues redefining New Jersey statehood as involving family connections. As she thinks back on her first term, she notes that it forms "a tapestry of faces. Families" ("Remarks" 2). She uses this address to illustrate three areas of the state that must be "rebuilt" in order to improve the "quality of life" of New Jersey families, so that they "are proud to call the Garden State home" (1). Rebuilding New Jersey is synonymous with rebuilding a home. She uses this opportunity to continue reworking the ideograph of statehood, now to include themes of family and "home," concentrating on what the state will mean to future generations. "Together, we can create a New Jersey we will be proud to pass on to our children and grandchildren. A New Jersey in which all our communities prosper. In which fertile farms, sparkling waters, and breathtaking mountain views remain lasting treasures. . . . Together, we can make New Jersey truly the Best Place to Live in America" (6). New Jersey is not only a family but also a home and living space that future generations will inhabit.

Her radio addresses are an interesting use of technology to overcome one difficulty of the New Jersey governorship, lack of media cohesion in rousing public opinion regarding New Jersey issues. New Jersey depends on Philadelphia and New York media markets, so the radio addresses are one way to secure local media attention. Howard Martin explains that President Ronald Reagan began to deliver a series of weekly radio addresses in 1982 that were evaluated as highly effective. The benefits of radio for Reagan were reaching an "auto-borne audience," "securing substantial attention from the same-day evening news reports," putting ideas and policy proposals on the public record, and setting the agenda for reporters and the legislature (Howard Martin 817–821).

Whitman's weekly radio addresses are an attempt to connect with the public in a similar fashion, creating a sense of unity with the public and giving the media elite, legislators, and individual citizens specific issues on which to focus discussion. According to a phone interview with Jim Hadden of the governor's communications staff, the governor's radio messages are prerecorded, and on Friday each week a "burst fax" is sent to all the media outlets in the tri-state area notifying them that the radio message is available. Approximately twenty to twenty-five calls are made each week by local media stations to record a copy of the address, which might be aired completely or in sound bytes. The governor's message is disseminated most widely through print media. The governor's office issues a press release in conjunction with the radio address, and many local weekly newspapers reprint the text of the address in their editorial section. Furthermore, her addresses are rebroadcast via "real audio" to anyone who has access to the Internet. Strategically, this added Internet function works to overcome the top-down perception of New Jersey politics through the use of the World Wide Web, allowing for listener participation and giving the listener and Web user a sense of control. Using the available technology demonstrates that the state's work is not isolated in Trenton but reaches out to include the people of the state geographically. The state appears concerned with connecting with its people, talking with them, and including them in the discussion of issues important to New Jersey. As a family, the state is person-oriented in that it solicits the input of each of its members.

Whitman's radio addresses work to redefine New Jersey statehood by expanding on three themes introduced in her second inaugural: open spaces, personal safety that comes from rebuilt neighborhoods and cities, and personal responsibility. And, she is able to connect each of these issues to the family and home that people have made in New Jersey. For example, New Jerseyans must preserve open spaces "for the sake of our families today and tomorrow" ("Open Space," 24 January 1998, 1). The State Plan, "a blueprint for a higher quality of life for us all," outlines a guide for developing the existing infrastructure and preserving open space so that New Jerseyans can spend more time "with your family each week" ("State" 1). Preserving New Jersey's open space "isn't just about preserving acres. . . . It's about maintaining the quality of life our families deserve—with clean air, clean water, and places to run around and have fun" ("Our Open Space" 2; paraphrased in "Open Space," 17 July 1998, 1–2; "Open Space" 9 October 1998, 1). Preserving New Jersey's open space is Whitman's "vision for a New Jersey that welcomes the 21st century with a lasting legacy of open space. A legacy of clean air and clean water. A legacy that keeps the Garden in the Garden State. A legacy that will make our grandchildren and their grandchildren proud to call New Jersey home" ("Our Open Space" 2). Preserving New Jersey's open space means preserving the home and the family. New Jersey statehood is redefined as openness and families. This resonates with Whitman's first inaugural pledge to "open" government to the people. Openness, along with family and home, becomes a sloganlike term included in the container that is "New Jersey."

Similarly, when discussing crime, Whitman focuses on issues of personal safety that are enhanced with better cities and neighborhoods, keeping the children, citizens, and families "of our great state" safe ("Crime" 2). This contributes to her statehood ideograph by redefining the state as a safe-haven, just like the home is a safe-haven. The container is broadened to include "neighborhood" and "community" while reinforcing the notion of family. Whitman is very proud of passing "Megan's Law," in order "to give parents a little more help in protecting their children . . . [and] to inform communities when convicted sex offenders move in" ("Mother's" 1). She explains that the "number of laws to help and protect domestic violence victims" exist so that mothers only have to worry about "the chores and challenges and miracles of motherhood" (2). Preventing crime promotes "better New Jersey" streets and neighborhoods and safer families ("Initiatives" 2). In her August 21, 1998, message, she discusses "Summer Safety," which concerns keeping your children safe when they are riding bicycles, traveling in vehicles, and spending time at the beach: "We can never be too careful when it comes to the safety of our families" ("Summer" 2). This goes for health care and schools too: "New Jersey KidCare" believes that "children deserve to enjoy the best of health. And that's what makes New Jersey special: we care enough to give our children the best" ("New Jersey KidCare" 2). And, Whitman announces a "collaborative approach to safe schools" in her September 11, 1998, message in which "parents, teachers, students, and school administrators" work together to prevent violence in schools. "We owe it to families to ensure that their children are safe when they get to school" ("School" 1). Protecting New Jersey means protecting not only New Jersey families but also New Jersey schools, another institution through which Whitman further broadens her control.

Finally, Whitman urges New Jerseyans to take personal responsibility for their actions, explaining that this will contribute to a better, safer society in which to raise our families. This is the topic of her first radio message and is repeated throughout 1998. Whitman explains what she calls a "crisis of personal responsibility" that can be solved only by reaching "out to all parts of society—families, neighborhoods, schools, companies, houses of worship, and even government" ("Personal Responsibility," 10 January 1998, 2). Many of these parts of society are institutions that, Althusser argues, function privately but must be controlled by the state in order to maintain power ideologically (110, 111, 117). Every "proud New Jerseyan" must practice personal responsibility when using New Jersey beaches, driving on New Jersey highways, and "in promoting responsible driving, responsible drinking, and lawful behavior" when enjoying the summer ("New Jersey Is Ready" 1). Personal responsibility also means "responsible family planning," which is "encouraged" through "New Jersey's family cap policies and welfare reform measures" ("Family" 1). As a result, "here in New Jersey, we are helping families improve their financial condition and helping all our children have the quality of life they deserve" (2). Personal responsibility gives people "one real power," according to Whitman, "the power to take full control of our lives" ("Personal Responsibility," 4 December 1998, 1). And, this responsibility must be "your lifelong goal to teach your children—and others—that behavior matters, that character counts, and that actions have consequences" (2). While giving "real power" to the people, Whitman also is extending her own power ideologically by appealing to the vulnerabilities and safety needs of the New Jersey family, justifying state protection.

At this moment in time, synchronically, Whitman uses New Jersey statehood to unite New Jerseyans' focus on specific issues that center on the family as well as other institutions such as the school and the Church. Furthermore, preserving the environment means more and better places for families to have fun. Safer streets and neighborhoods mean safer families. And, teaching personal responsibility in the home contributes to safer streets and neighborhoods. Throughout Whitman's inaugurals and her radio addresses, she emphasizes *our, we*, and *us,* government and localities working together like a family. The state becomes connected with its citizens because each has a voice in "reinventing" and "rebuilding" New Jersey. New Jersey becomes synonymous with family, suggesting closeness through interconnection among all citizens.

THE PEOPLE

Even though Whitman builds her vision of New Jersey statehood as one that focuses on family and home, synchronically the ideograph of New Jersey statehood has to compete with masculine conceptions of state power, competition, and control. However, her use of a private sphere, or traditionally "feminine" thematic, is not yet enough to foster an ideological change. Whitman's enactment of ideology is further illustrated by examining how she constructs rhetorically "the people" of the state. McGee explains the rhetorical formation of "the people" as a collectivization process ("In Search" 243). "The people" are created as "reality," remain as long as the rhetoric is in force, and fade away into "a collection of individuals" (242). "The people" are created when leaders organize their ideological commitments into political myths, assuming a people who can affect reality. Collective identity exists, "not in a single myth, but in the *competitive relationships* which develop between a myth and objective reality, and between a myth and antithetical visions of the collective life" (246). Whitman creates "the people" through her use of the ideograph of New Jersey statehood, which incorporates the stable myth of masculine tradition and a rhetoric of control along with the vital myth of family, diversity, and traditionally "feminine" issues motivating consensus building, collaboration, and inclusion.

Whitman's "people" are a heterogeneous collection from "the factories of Paterson and the research laboratories of Princeton," "ethnic neighborhoods," "senior citizen villages," "towns . . . and cities" ("Inaugural"). Despite their differing ages, racial backgrounds, and economic classes, New Jersey's "people" are united as "one family, one community, one state" (9). When one fails, all fail; "when we help one another succeed, we all succeed" (10). Emphasis is placed on collectivity and collective agency over the individual in order to bolster activism and motivation, showing "the world what New Jersey can do" (10). These various individuals are united strategically within their "one state" of New Jersey. New Jersey is not only a place, but it is also used ideographically as a family. If all of these faces are found within the place, they are also located within the family, called into existence in order to advance Whitman's ideology. As a result, they become not a collection of individuals but a collective.

The second inaugural continues this theme, calling a diverse people into a unity that Whitman defines as "Many Faces, One Family." After establishing the unity of these individuals and their force as a collective, Whitman uses these faces to illustrate the leadership work that comes from the New Jersey family. She occasionally mentions individuals by name: "Amelia Rocto-James and Michael James," who own a restaurant that is sure to flourish with the opening of the Performing Arts Center in Newark ("Remarks" 2). She lists other "everyday heroes" as examples of the people who make up New Jersey and who provide leadership by their example: "neighbor helping neighbor after a pipeline exploded in Edison . . . a 12–year-old who spent 80 hours selling lemonade to raise money for the victims of Oklahoma City . . . mothers working their way off welfare and business people giving them that chance . . . great teachers [who] inspire students . . . [and] our state's finest who gave their lives to protect us all" (7). As Karlyn Kohrs Campbell explains, one of the attributes of "feminine style" is the development of credibility and authority by example, a characteristic often found in the rhetoric of the early suffragists (*Man*, 1: 12–13). As Whitman calls a variety of individuals into existence as "the people," she does so in a manner gendered feminine, thus highlighting the vital myth of feminine inclusion. Similarly, Whitman includes herself as "just one of the Many Faces of our One Family" to read for Recordings for the Blind and Dyslexic, thus demonstrating "leadership by example" in motivating "the people" "to improve the quality of life" of the New Jersey family ("Remarks" 6–7).

Whitman closes her second inaugural with: "Fellow New Jerseyans, eight million strong: you are a great, free, happy, and intelligent people. You are a thoughtful and generous people. You cherish our liberty. You enrich our prosperity. And I am deeply proud to serve you as Governor" (7). "The people" are hailed as thoughtful and active, making a difference for New Jersey's future. And, this is clearly where Whitman wants the emphasis as she talks of developing safer cities, "preserving our open space, and enriching our sense of personal responsibility" (2), the three planks of her second inaugural. Yet, calling the people thoughtful and active does not necessarily mean they are in practice.

Whitman's radio addresses continue the process by mentioning more of New Jersey's people, highlighting the diversity of people who make up the state family. For example, her January 17, 1998, address, "Celebrating the Best of New Jersey," recounts the tireless efforts of everyone from sports figures to "a boy from Trenton" who make up "some of the many reasons we are so proud to call New Jersey home" (1). Not only do these individuals provide leadership by example but they also make up the person-oriented family that is New Jersey. In her April 4, 1998, address on "Keeping Our Community Colleges Strong," she lists many whose "determination to get an education" inspire her, like the "single mother who works, cares for her children, and *still* manages to attend" (1). In Memorial Day and Veteran's Day addresses, Whitman commemorates the "New Jersey patriots [who] gave to our nation in time of war" ("Remembering" 1); we must continue to remember their "stirring legacy of leadership, patriotism, and courage" ("Serving" 2). During the "July 4th" address she recounts what she calls "the promise of America": Many immigrants "chose New Jersey as their home" and contribute to the "endless opportunities to appreciate" different cultures, music, art, food, sports, and more (1). New Jersey's people are "leaders in every field of endeavor," ranging "from Woodrow Wilson to Millicent Fenwick, Thomas Edison to Albert Einstein, Frank Sinatra to Bruce Springsteen, Walt Whitman to Joyce Carol Oates, Jersey Joe Walcott to Althea Gibson" (1). She doesn't forget New Jersey's senior citizens either, noting their contributions in her August 7, 1998, address, "Services for Seniors." She explains that "our older citizens are an extremely diverse group, defined not by their birthdates but by their values, experiences, and lifestyles" (1). Furthermore, Whitman delivered an address from Mexico while on a trade mission there in September and recalled, "Many of the Faces in our One Family are of Mexican heritage. . . . I'm committed to helping our one family find its place in the truly global family of the 21st century" ("Business" 2).

All of these faces make up the diversity that is "the people" of New Jersey. In an effort to celebrate this diversity, her October 2, 1998, address, "Many Faces, One Family," "sum[s] up how I feel about the people I am so proud to serve as Governor of New Jersey" (1). The address also publicizes "Many Faces, One Family Week," a time during which New Jersey's families can take part in events and activities statewide, "sharing the many traditions and cultures from which we draw strength and vitality" (1). The events also warrant their own Web site: http:/www. state.nj. us/state/secretar/faces/facesidx.html. This address most clearly captures "the people," the collective identity that Whitman activates during her term in office through the vital feminine myth of family, diversity, and inclusion: "We come from so many different backgrounds and cultures. We speak so many languages, celebrate so many faiths, and carry on so many traditions. Yet we all share a common humanity, a common residence, and a common desire for New Jersey to be the best state in which to live, work, and raise a family" (1). Furthermore, Whitman explains that an appreciation for "our common humanity" makes us better equipped to build "a state of harmony and respect . . . a place where people come together and look after one another . . . a place where solace and strength are as close as the person standing next to you . . . just like in a family" (1).

Whitman unites diversity by emphasizing the "common humanity" of New Jerseyans. Brown explains that liberalism focuses on equality "as a condition of sameness, a condition in which humans share the same nature, the same rights, and the same terms of regard by state institutions" (*States* 153). However, one problem with this is that "injustice occurs when those considered the same are treated differently" (153). Brown argues that liberalism is founded on the equality of humanity; however, this equality has evolved as a gendered equality, "because it secures gender privilege through naming women as different and men as the neutral standard of the same" (153). The result is to reify gender difference and masculinity as the norm. Even while she attempts to use gender-neutral language, Whitman reinforces masculinity's privilege by uniting "the people" under the common sameness of "humanity" without also questioning how that sameness is premised, by differentiation from women, people of color, homosexuality, and so on.

Furthermore, it is clear that all those who make up New Jersey's family are not equal. The content of Whitman's addresses that brings presence and visibility to the people must not overshadow the way these aspects are used. According to Whitman, democracy is practiced when government "trust[s] and listen[s] to the people" and is defined by institutions such as the economic system, the educational system, and the criminal justice system, all systems that Whitman says must be "reinvented" in order for New Jersey to "lead the nation" ("Inaugural"). Whitman's vision places democracy at the level of the institution, not at the level of "the people." If Whitman's New Jersey is indeed a family, then it functions as a hierarchical family, in which the government-as-parent dictates and controls the people-as-children. New Jersey's "One Family" as ideograph is an attempt to mask the hierarchy implicit in such a metaphor. It is a family that reinvents the parent's authority, not the children's or even the family as a whole. While these children are framed as having a voice, they are also framed as limited in their power inasmuch as the emphasis is placed on institutions: the "economic engine," competitive businesses, and "a strong core curriculum" in schools that "demand discipline" ("Inaugural" 2, 4, 6–9). While the children may be encouraged to speak, the parental institutions are the real actors and the children speak only when spoken to. Yet, the factor of calling attention to the visibility of New Jersey citizens and declaring them thoughtful and active relies on the logic of the norm of objectivity—naming something in a particular way makes it so—whether it is or not. Democracy is appealed to in name only, not in practice.

Whitman's "people" is a collectivity that has a dependent relationship with government that fulfills needs rather than grants rights. Brown explains that "it is a commonplace of liberalism that rights pertain to civil society while needs govern the family" (*States* 159). Furthermore, rights actualize liberty, while needs are the effect of encumbrance, permitting "legitimate inequalities based upon 'differences': for example, those between children and parents, women and men. . . . Rights relations presume autonomy and independence while relations of need presume intimacy and dependence" (Brown, *States* 159). Whitman's "people," past and future, are dependent on state services ("Remarks" 6), "workers" for the state (7), pawns at the mercy of government (6), and families encumbered with raising children (8). Whitman's family metaphor is simply another system that "the people" are a part of, making it difficult to break free of the constraints that have been defined diachronically. Even though Whitman articulates family themes, thus private-sphere values, with public or political ideology, it is a mistake to assume that she has completely freed herself and her people from the time-honored constraints of liberal democracy. Her discourse calls into being "the people" defined by liberalism's control. The rhetorical implications are that a "people" become feminized and dependent upon the socially masculine, institutional structure, which is legitimated by the rational norms guiding New Jersey's political ideology.

Her radio addresses are constant announcements for more government programs designed to protect, preserve, maintain, secure, or defend. New Jersey is all about masculine entailments motivating control—legislation for this and legislation for that—perhaps because of the power of the governorship. Control is built into its very nature constitutionally and legitimated each time more legislation is passed. Leaders and citizens alike are lulled into a sense of normalcy when choice, freedom, and inclusion are legislated. Thus, the basic ideological structure is held consonant.

McGee explains that the power of the ideograph is not in its content but in its usage ("Ideograph" 10). Whitman's public motives are strength, power, and hierarchy as found in a traditional, positional family structure. Her use of "New Jersey" as an ideograph simply works to reinscribe gender relations while giving the impression of being more inclusive and family-friendly. Furthermore, Charland argues that when examining ideological rhetoric, we must notice not only the "arguments and ideographs, but . . . the very nature of the subjects that rhetoric both addresses and leads to come to be" (148). Even though Whitman addresses families and a diverse "people" in a way that appears more inclusive and different from that of previous governors, she "establishes the boundary of [the] subject's motives and experience" in a fashion similar to the past: "A transformed ideology would require a transformed subject" (Charland 148). In Whitman's case, we have neither.

Time-Space Distanciation

Whitman reinforces liberalism's control through her use of the ideograph of New Jersey statehood and her definition of "the people." Finally, and perhaps most compellingly, Whitman's ideological structure is demonstrated through Anthony Giddens's explanation of time-space relations found in capitalist societies. Giddens explains time-space relations in capitalist societies in conjunction with power (29–30). He theorizes power, not as power over, but as centrally related to freedom and human action. Time, structure, and space bind all social activity: "The conjunction of these express[es] the *situated* character of social practices. The 'binding' of time and space in social systems *always* has to be examined historically, in terms of the bounded knowledgeability of human action" (Giddens 30).

Giddens argues that the structuration of capitalist societies occurs in time-space through "time-space distanciation," best explained by contrasting capitalist societies with smaller hunter-gatherer (noncapitalist) societies. In noncapitalist societies, time-space distanciation occurs through legitimization by tradition and through the role played by kinship in structuring social relations. What is important here is "high presence-availability" (100–101). Social transactions occur face-to-face, and tradition is the expression of the human memory of continuing social practices found in oral societies. Human memory is the "storage container" of authoritative resources, or the material necessary to legitimize power (Giddens 146–147). By contrast, capitalist societies are characterized by "low presence-availability," by absence rather than presence. The source of legitimization is no longer tradition but the day-to-day routinization of activities, knowledge of which is stored in institutional formations such as the community, the city (early capitalism), or the state by means of surveillance. Furthermore, time and space become commodities. Time is separated from lived experience and thought of as pure or formless, while space is not localized and is thought of as created. Thus, there is a high level of "time-space distanciation" in capitalist societies (Giddens 156).

If Whitman truly reinvents state government to be more open, inclusive, and listener focused (her goal as stated in her first inaugural), then it follows that there will be "high presence-availability" to her discourse, challenging the ideological structure of the New Jersey governorship. Whitman's use of time-space relations certainly negotiates between presence and absence. Whitman begins her first inaugural by acknowledging two aspects of tradition: (1) the former Democratic governor and (2) her family. In thanking "Governor Florio for his years of public service," Whitman states that she had occasion to both agree and disagree with her predecessor (1). Thus, she invokes his name not for its authority value but simply as a marker in time, as "a proud moment . . . [and] a humbling moment" (1). This moment in time identifies a lived experience that will serve as a frame for her experiences in the governorship. Additionally, Whitman thanks her family, her "husband John and [her] two children, Kate and Taylor, for standing by" during the campaign (1). These faces are visibly present in the audience and have been present throughout the campaign. Furthermore, they serve as a metaphor for Whitman's inaugural theme of "New Jersey, One Family," strategically relying on kinship ties to set her ideology in motion. By invoking New Jersey statehood as a family, she is able to unite her "people" in space and time. She focuses on the experience of the moment but also "creates" a space that includes her real-life family and her New Jersey family as well as earlier generations in time who fought "at the forefront of a revolution" in 1776 (10).

The notion of presence and living connection is reinforced through Whitman's second inaugural and radio addresses. In a similar fashion, she opens her second inaugural by thanking her family by name and referring to a former Republican governor, this time invoking his name for its authority value. She thanks "Tom for giving me encouragement and advice four years ago when, like him, I was elected to my first term by the slimmest of margins" ("Remarks" 1). Former governor Kean is present in the audience. Also, specific examples of New Jersey's "everyday heroes" are present in Whitman's discourse, noting "leadership by example" ("Remarks" 6–7). As a result she gives presence to the many faces in New Jersey's family.

These specific instances are carried throughout those radio addresses in which she uses the opportunity to mention numerous "everyday heroes": "Celebrating the Best of New Jersey," "Keeping Our Community Colleges Strong," "Mother's Day," "Remembering Our Fallen Heroes," "July 4th," "Many Faces, One Family," "Serving New Jersey's Veterans," and "Iraq Military Mission." Each of these addresses emphasizes the lived experiences of the individuals who make up New Jersey's family, reinforcing Giddens' concept of "high presence-availability."

However, the use of radio broadcasting and "real audio" complicates the presence achieved by these examples. Whitman's words are prerecorded, never delivered live to the public. Certainly, New Jersey's location between New York and Philadelphia media markets makes this a necessity; however, it also creates a false sense of connection between Whitman and her public. Additionally, Internet access makes Whitman's words present anytime the user demands. However, this presence is created, pure, and formless rather than something that occurs in real time. Rather than forming specific boundaries for localized human activity, time and space are manipulated, used, and created.

Presence and absence become further complicated in Whitman's concern for New Jersey's legacy, the collective memory that the New Jersey family possesses and uses to legitimate future actions. Whitman's radio addresses outline the legacy she hopes to leave for the future of New Jersey: "Working together, we can employ old-fashioned values as living, vibrant ideals to guide us in creating the kind of society we will feel proud to leave to our children and grandchildren" ("Personal Responsibility,"10 January 1998, 2). Whitman calls on tradition to guide the way to the future. Whitman's October address on "Historic Preservation" outlines "Public Question No. 1," a voting issue through which the citizens can "literally shape the landscape of our future . . . [by] preserving our history" (1). Whitman lists numerous parks, historic homes, a courthouse, battle sites, and other places that are important to preserving "the charm and beauty and style of our heritage. Restoring and preserving these pieces of our history makes our neighborhoods and communities more attractive places in which to live and work and raise a family" (2). Here, history is not remembered, but a particular history is created and preserved through government legislation. This is true of the "open space initiative" as well. In Whitman's November 28 address, she thanks the public for "recognizing the importance of protecting the environment before it is too late. This is our legacy to future generations. It will make New Jersey an even better place in which to live, work, and raise a family" ("Thanksgiving" 1). The day-to-day routine of living, working, and raising a family legitimates the practice of saving open space and preserving historic sites. Saving and preserving are not done for the sake of human memories passed down through the kinship relations of New Jersey's family.

Whitman attempts to "create" high presence-availability through the "lasting legacy of open space. A legacy of clean air and clean water . . . a legacy that will make our grandchildren and their grandchildren proud to call New Jersey home" ("Our Open Space" 2; paraphrased in "Open Space" 17 July 1998, 1–2; "TTF" 2; "Open Space" 9 October 1998, 2; "One Million" 1). However, the very nature of "created" space is problematic in that land becomes a commodity that must be protected by government institutions: "Together, we can win the space race—the open space race. Together, we can build a sustainable society—a society in which we take care of the resources we have today so that they are there for us to enjoy tomorrow" ("Open Space" 24 January 1998, 2). In Whitman's second inaugural, she explained her goal of preserving one million acres of open space. In a radio message titled "Environment," she makes "a down payment on this pledge" (1). Clearly, space is a commodity to be acquired and developed appropriately; therefore, the "State Plan" message outlines procedures to accomplish this end: "Perhaps it will mean that the open space in your town won't become a strip mall or an office building but will remain a natural beauty or become a park for everyone to enjoy. Perhaps it will mean that the abandoned buildings in your downtown will be reclaimed, refurbished, and re-occupied by new businesses or new neighbors" (2). According to Whitman, preserving open space is "a great down payment on our quality of life" ("Earth" 2; paraphrased in "Our Open Space" 1).

Furthermore, Whitman's discussion of "Tourism" emphasizes the commodity value of New Jersey's space. Tourism, "the state's second largest industry . . . employs more than 623,000 men and women in good jobs, with a total payroll of $13 billion" ("Tourism" 1). And, New Jersey's "economy depends on tourism" ("New Jersey Is Ready" 1). Whitman also announces "a return to our state's most beloved tourism slogan: New Jersey & You . . . Perfect Together" ("Tourism" 1). Continued use of this slogan and its variations reinforces the commodity value of New Jersey spaces. For example, Whitman explains in her September 4 address, titled "Autumn Tourism," that "Autumn is possibly the most beautiful time to visit New Jersey's great outdoors. With more than 800 lakes and ponds, over 6000 miles of rivers, and one million acres of pine forests, there is sure to be something for everyone" (1). After all, "New Jersey and fall vacation plans are perfect together" (2).

As a result, space becomes a commodity that must be preserved by government legislation, and such preservation is legitimated through the routine workings of day-to-day life. New Jersey's "people" are viewed not as present, active, thoughtful decision-makers whose memory legitimates future actions but as dependent on government institutions that sanction decision making. For example, in order to rebuild cities, Whitman proposes "legislation that enables cities to acquire and redevelop these properties" ("Remarks" 3). City planning commissions, not local community groups, do the work. Furthermore, Whitman proposes a "Faith-Based Community Development Initiative" to offer job training and child care support so that communities can be rebuilt. However, this "community" initiative is not in cooperation with neighborhoods or local churches, but with businesses and religious institutions ("Remarks" 3). Clearly, improvement works from the top down, not from the level of the individual. Thus, "the people" are lost or absent from the democratic workings of local improvement efforts. The significance of this move is not in the fact that Whitman is being practical, for how else could things be accomplished if not for elected representatives and government mandates. The significance is that "the people" are strategically called upon as active and present, but in practice they are absent. Democracy works in name only, reinforcing the "low presence-availability," which is found in capitalist societies.

Similarly, development issues are purportedly given back to localities, suggesting "high presence-availability" in decision making. However, Whitman proposes to "give towns a guidebook to determine the true costs and benefits of a developer's proposal" ("Remarks" 4). Whitman promises that state government will "pledge to get out of your way"—as long as the development decisions you do make are "in concert with the State Plan" (4). Under the guise of getting localities involved in local decision making, giving the choice back to the people, state government still dictates how decisions are made. Democracy lies at the level of government institutions, not at the level of the people. Perhaps this is most clearly illustrated when Whitman states: "We'll let you know about things that matter to you: the quality of our water, the status of our cities, the traffic on our streets, the health of our children. And we'll tell you just how we're doing . . . good, bad, or ugly" ("Remarks" 6). Strategically, government control is imposed, dictates the agenda of things that matter, and separates the public from the workings of government while at the same time the "people" are constructed as present in the decision through the use of the word *our* and their visibility throughout Whitman's addresses. Whitman further states: "You deserve to know" ("Remarks" 6). She doesn't say the public deserves to make its own decisions. It is only important that the people know what government wants them to know and speak when told the important issues of concern. This is how New Jersey's "people" become unified and are ostensibly given a voice in state government.

The "common residence" of New Jerseyans functions as a uniting force as well. As Whitman states in her "Many Faces, One Family" address, "we all share a common humanity, a common residence, and a common desire for New Jersey to be the best state in which to live, work, and raise a family" (1). Created space becomes the emphasis over real localities in which productive deliberation takes place. "New Jersey" as ideograph calling into existence an absent "people" unifies Whitman's ideology. The collective, both space and people, is constructed as in need of protection, being told what issues to talk about, dependent, thus feminized, and necessitating masculine control through government initiatives and programs that come to their aid, instituted by the state apparatus, the level at which democracy works.

CONCLUSIONS

By examining the ideograph of statehood, the construction of "the people," and time-space relations in each inaugural and the first year of her radio addresses, we have a specific example of how Christine Todd Whitman sets her ideology in motion. In her inaugurals and radio addresses, Whitman enacts her version of liberal democracy that defines her use of power as New Jersey's governor. She uses "New Jersey" ideographically to create a less active "people" united in space-time structuration. Whereas Whitman's articulation does put more money in the pockets of her people, the overall changes are merely cosmetic, a reinvention of the very structures of authority. Liberalism for Whitman is clearly concerned with maintaining government power through a government "reinvented" in its own image. Whitman collectively defined the people via negotiation of the myth of masculine control and the myth of feminine inclusion and diversity. Even though Whitman relies on feminine thematics in her discourse, these do not change the underlying ideological structure of the governorship. While Whitman attempts to negotiate space-time relations, the faces of the people are constructed as absent from the work that must be done to reinvent New Jersey's government. Yet the family metaphor, the numerous examples of leadership by example, and the presence of Whitman's own family at her inaugurals mask such absence.

By engaging the political discourse through which Christine Todd Whitman negotiates the governorship of New Jersey, what becomes apparent is the following: Whitman's discourse relies heavily on traditionally feminine content such as diversity and the family in order to put her ideology in motion. She has high hopes to reinvent government, not in its own control-oriented image, but in a more inclusive image that restores power to the level of the people. Redefining New Jersey ideographically as a family is one step in this direction. However, we cannot simply focus on the content of her discourse. McGee tells us to focus on her usage of ideographs. Thus, the ideograph of statehood is used to define New Jersey's "people" as taking part in a particular type of family structure. Structurally, the traditional family is not person-oriented and decisions are not made via consensus. Instead, the "people" are called into being as having less decision making power than those in government. If New Jersey is a family, then "the people" are its children. Charland tells us that if ideology is to change, subject positions must also change. This is not the case in New Jersey. "The people" have the same dependent relationship with government that they have always had. However, things are structured in such a way as to imply more power on the part of the people. The family of New Jersey appears united in time and space as they share a "common residence" with their governor who delivers weekly messages directly to them. However, there is no "real time" to her messages. The use of radio and Internet technology creates a sense of presence that is not really there. Furthermore, when it comes to decision-making that truly influences the workings of the state, the people are absent there as well. Localities make decisions under the dictates of the State Plan, or in conjunction with businesses, not in conjunction with community groups. Democracy is appealed to in name only, not in practice.

Thus, the ideological content of Whitman's discourse manifests itself through her control-oriented, top-down construction of government institutions that do the real decision-making work. She produces a hegemonic articulation that gives the impression of moving forward productively while offering no structural change. As a result, she reinscribes gender relations without broadening the boundaries for political decision making. The people remain dependent, thus feminized, and the family and diversity, traditionally feminine concerns, remain marginalized in the realm of the feminine. The real work of government maintains its masculine-control structure and perpetuates itself throughout her term. Perhaps this is why Whitman's gender is rarely the subject of controversy in state politics. Ideologically, she enacts the masculine norms legitimized time and again in New Jersey. As a result, she finds herself in a powerful position of leadership, reinforced through re-election, and a formidable contender for a future national office. While Whitman proves that a woman can enact leadership powerfully and competently, she does so in a manner that does not change the gendered boundaries of political power in a liberal democracy; it only reinforces them.

Conclusion

While the personal perspectives and methods of analysis of each of the contributing authors reflect the diversity evident in the personalities, rhetorical styles, and obstacles faced by each of the women governors, several common themes emerge. An issue that permeates each of these studies is the Western notion of a public-and-private sphere duality that each of the women in this study struggled to overcome. Simply by being elected, these women debunked the prevailing attitude that women belonged in the home, not the statehouse. However, merely acquiring the position does not guarantee unlimited political success. In fact, women must constantly prove their worth and maintain their credibility in the face of political boundaries grounded in the public-private dichotomy.

As these women have navigated the boundaries between the public and the private spheres, they have not only resculptured the face of the governorship but they have redefined women's roles. For instance, Nellie Tayloe Ross attempted to maintain a delicate balance between her public role as governor and her private role as woman and mother. Although she advocated for women's participation in politics, she was careful not to upset the prevailing notions of femininity. Likewise, the women governors of the 1990s worked within the traditional societal constructs for womanhood yet at the same time contributed to the creation of new paradigms that redefined female roles and suggested that woman's place is in both the women's sphere and in the public arena.

Once women enter the governorship, they essentially restructure the political landscape. The woman governors discussed in the preceding chapters brought issues of caring, personal experience, empowerment, family, and inclusivity to the statehouse. These issues contrast sharply with traditional, male-centered ideologies and give renewed vigor to a revised moral point of view in contemporary politics.

Each of the women in this study envisioned a government of, by, and for the people in both philosophical and pragmatic terms. They sought to create a government that encompassed the views of the citizenry and that was responsible to citizens' wishes. They opened the doors of the statehouse to their publics and opened their ears to the appeals set before them. While not all of the women enjoyed success in their endeavor to craft a shared government, they all believed that the attempt was worthy of their efforts.

No matter what these governors believed in or what they attempted, their success or failure hinged on their ability to operate from appropriate rhetorical constructs and to use effective discourse strategies to navigate the political boundaries they encountered. Some, like Ann Richards, used vivid images and strong emotional appeals to reach a public unaccustomed to female leadership. Conversely, Barbara Roberts was unable to compose a message that would resonate with her audience despite her vision for the state. The totality of experiences of the five women studied in this book instructs us that because of political double binds, women must both re-vision and re-frame political boundaries. Skillful rhetorical navigation of these boundaries is crucial for success in electoral politics.

We began this study with the belief that there was a lack of analysis of the rhetoric of women governors. Our research has confirmed this. Interestingly, we have found little scholarly attention given to the role of the governor in general despite the fact that, except for the presidency, the governor is the most powerful elected official in the country. Women in the United States continue to change the gubernatorial landscape and contribute to the increasing importance of this role at both the state and the federal levels. Thus, the values and perspectives revealed in their discourse must merit our further investigation.

Works Consulted

"AEC Gets a Female Boss." *Senior Scholastic* 5 Mar. 1973: 17.

Alexander, Shana. "On the Lookout for Lurleen." *Life* 22 July 1966: 19.

Althusser, Louis. "Ideology and Ideological State Apparatuses: Notes towards an Investigation." *Mapping Ideology.* Ed. Slavoj Žižek. New York: Verso, 1994. 100–140.

Anderson, Judith. *Outspoken Women: Speeches by American Reformers, 1635–1936.* Dubuque, IA: Kendall, 1984.

Aranya, Nissim, Talma. Kushnir, and Aharon Valency. "Organizational Commitment in Male-Dominated Professions." *Human Relations* 39 (1986): 433–448.

"Arizona Race in Turmoil as Governor Bows Out." *New York Times* 21 January 1990, Sun. late ed., sec. 1: 24. Online. Lexis-Nexis, Academic Universe. 27 September 1999.

Ayres, B. Drummond Jr. "Whitman, in California, Fields the Vice-Presidency Question." *New York Times* 30 April 1995, late ed., sec. 1: 37.

Barge, J. Kevin. *Leadership: Communication Skills for Organizations and Groups.* New York: St. Martin's, 1994.

Behn, Robert D. "Getting the Job Done: The Governor's Legal and Moral Authority." *Journal of State Government* 59.2 (1986): 54–57.

Bem, Sandra Lipsitz. *The Lenses of Gender.* New Haven: Yale UP, 1993.

Bentley, Max. " 'I'll Be Governor, Not Jim,' Says Ma Ferguson." *Collier's* 27 Sept. 1924: 12.

Beyle, Thad. "Being Governor." *The State of the States.* 2nd ed. Ed. Carl E. Van Horn. Washington, DC: Congressional Quarterly Press 1993. 79–113.

———, and Lynn Muchmore. *Being Governor.* Durham, NC: Duke UP, 1983.

Biesecker, Barbara. "Coming to Terms with Recent Attempts to Write Women into the History of Rhetoric." *Rethinking the History of Rhetoric: Multidisciplinary Essays on the Rhetorical Tradition*. Ed. Takous Poulakos. San Francisco: Westview Press, 1992. 153–172.

Bizzell, Patricia, and Bruce Herzberg. *The Rhetorical Tradition: Rhetoric from Classical Times to the Present*. Boston: Bedford, 1990.

Blackford, Linda B. "National Test Puts Ky. Near Top in Reading Gains." *Lexington Herald-Leader* 5 Mar. 1999, metro final ed.: A1+.

Blankenship, Jane, and Deborah C. Robson. "A 'Feminine Style' in Women's Political Discourse: An Exploratory Essay." *Communication Quarterly* 43 (1995): 353–366.

Boardman, Fon W. *America in the Gilded Age: 1876–1900*. New York: Walack, 1972.

Bolman, Lee G., and Terrence E. Deal. *Reframing Organizations: Artistry, Choice, and Leadership*. 2nd ed. San Francisco: Jossey-Bass, 1997.

Bools, Barbara, and Lydia Swan. *Power Failure: Why Some Women Short Circuit Their Careers and How to Avoid It*. New York: St. Martin's, 1989.

Braden, Waldo, ed. *Oratory in the New South*. Baton Rouge: Louisiana State UP, 1979.

Brigance, W. Norwood, ed. *A History and Criticism of American Public Address*. 2 vols. New York: McGraw-Hill, 1943. New York: Russell & Russell, 1960.

Brill, Alida, ed. *A Rising Public Voice: Women in Politics Worldwide*. New York: Feminist Press-City University of New York, 1995.

Broudy, Harry S. *Truth and Credibility: The Citizen's Dilemma*. New York: Longman, 1981.

Brown, Wendy. *Manhood and Politics: A Feminist Reading in Political Theory*. Totowa, NJ: Rowman and Littlefield, 1988.

———. *States of Injury: Power and Freedom in Late Modernity*. Princeton, NJ: Princeton UP, 1995.

Burke, Kenneth. *Attitudes toward History*. 3rd ed. Berkeley: U of California P, 1984.

———. *A Rhetoric of Motives*. Berkeley: U of California P, 1969.

Burkholder, Thomas R. "Mary Clyens Lease (1850–1933) 'Raising Hell' for Populism and Woman's Rights." *Woman Public Speakers in the United States, 1800–1925: A Bio-Critical Sourcebook*. Ed. Karlyn Kohrs Campbell. Westport, CT: Greenwood, 1993. 111–124.

———. "Kansas Populism, Woman Suffrage, and the Agrarian Myth: A Case Study in the Limits of Mythic Transcendence." *Communication Studies* 40 (1989): 292–307.

———. "Mythic Conflict: A Critical Analysis of Kansas Populist Speechmaking, 1890–1894." Unpublished Diss. U of Kansas, 1988.

Burnham, Alexander. "Governor Grasso's Troubles." *Progressive* Jan. 1978: 36–37.

———. "The Testing of Ella Grasso." *Progressive* April 1976: 34–36.

Campbell, Karlyn Kohrs. *Man Cannot Speak for Her: A Critical Study of Early Feminist Rhetoric.* Vol. 1. New York: Praeger, 1989.

———, comp. *Man Cannot Speak for Her: Key Texts of the Early Feminists.* Vol. 2. New York: Praeger, 1989.

———. "The Rhetoric of Women's Liberation: An Oxymoron." *Quarterly Journal of Speech* 59 (1973): 74–86.

———. "Stanton's 'The Solitude of Self': A Rationale for Feminism. "*Quarterly Journal of Speech* 66 (1980): 304–312.

———. "Style and Content in the Rhetoric of Early Afro-American Feminists." *Quarterly Journal of Speech* 72 (1986): 434–445.

———, ed. *Women Public Speakers in the United States, 1800–1925: A Bio-Critical Sourcebook.* Westport, CT: Greenwood, 1993.

———, ed. *Women Public Speakers in the United States, 1925–1993: A Bio-Critical Sourcebook.* Westport, CT: Greenwood, 1994.

———, and E. Claire Jerry. "Woman and Speaker: A Conflict in Roles." *Seeing Female: Social Roles and Personal Lives.* Ed. Sharon S. Brehm. Westport, CT: Greenwood, 1988. 123–133.

Cantor, Dorothy W., and Toni Bernay. *Women in Power: The Secret of Leadership.* Boston: Houghton, 1992.

Carlson, A. Cheree. "Defining Womanhood: Lucretia Mott and the Transformation of Femininity." *Western Journal of Communication* 58.2 (1994): 85–97.

Carroll, Susan J. *Women as Candidates in American Politics.* 2nd ed. Bloomington, IN: Indiana UP, 1994.

Charland, Maurice. "Constitutive Rhetoric: The Case of the *Peuple Québécois.*" *Quarterly Journal of Speech* 73 (1987): 133–150.

Chorpening, Jennifer. "Hollister Signs Bill to Preserve Farmland." *Dayton Daily News* 5 Jan. 1999, city ed.: 6B. Online. Lexis-Nexis, Academic Universe. 3 September 1999.

"Christine Todd Whitman: Biography." Office of the Governor. 10 June 1998. <http://www.state.nj.us/governor/ctwbio.html>.

"Christine Whitman Seen as Vice Presidential Material." *Chicago Tribune* 25 Jan. 1995, evening update ed., sec. News: 2. Chicago Tribune Company. Online. Lexis-Nexis. 20 Oct. 1998.

Chu, Daniel, with William J. Cook. "Governors: Whistling Dixy." *Newsweek* 4 Oct. 1976: 47.

Coleman, Ronald G. "Suffrage and Prohibition: Integrated Issues." *America in Controversy: History of American Public Address.* Ed. DeWitte Holland. Dubuque, IA: Wm. C. Brown, 1973. 261–279.

Collins, Eliza G. C. *"Dearest Amanda . . .": An Executives's Advice to Her Daughter.* New York: Harper, 1984.

"Collins, Martha Layne." *Current Biography.* Ed. Charles Moritz. Vol. 47. New York: Wilson, 1986, 1987. 91–94.

Collins, Martha Layne. "Address to Special Session of Legislature." Rec. 8 July 1984. Videotape. Kentucky Educational Television, Frankfort, KY. KET Archives.

Collins, Martha Layne. "A Major Policy Address." Rec. 15 Mar. 1984. Videotape. Kentucky Educational Television, Lexington, KY. KET Archives.

Collins, Martha Layne. Personal interviews. 1991–1999.

Collins, Martha Layne. "State of the Commonwealth Address." Rec. 15 Jan. 1984. Videotape. Kentucky Educational Television, Frankfort, KY. KET Archives.

"Connecticut's Favorite Daughter: Ella T. Grasso, 1919–1981." *Time* 16 Feb. 1981: 20.

Cook, Allison. "Lone Star." *New York Times Magazine* 7 Feb. 1993: 24–47.

Cox, Raymond W. III. *Intergovernmental Relations as an Instrument of Policy Change*. Washington, DC: National Science Foundation, 1984.

Crouch, Ronald. Kentucky State Data Center. University of Louisville. Telephone Interview. 20 October 1998.

"Cynthia Jeanne Shaheen." AP Candidate Bios. 7 Nov. 1996. *Associated Press Political Service*. Online. Lexis-Nexis. 20 Oct. 1998.

"Defeat for Dixy Lee Ray." *Time* 29 Sept. 1980: 25.

DeFrancisco, Victoria L., and Marvin D. Jensen, eds. *Women's Voices in Our Time: Statements by American Leaders*. Prospect Heights, IL: Waveland, 1994.

"Dixy Lee Ray, Former Head of U.S. Atomic Agency, Dies." *Los Angeles Times* 3 Jan. 1994, home ed.: A3.

"Dixy Rocks the Northwest." *Time* 12 Dec. 1977: 26–29+.

Doan, Michael, and Michael Bosc. "Kay Orr and Helen Boosalis: Woman Power on the Prairie." *U.S. News &World Report* 26 May 1986: 8.

Dobris, Catherine A. "In the Year of Big Sister: Toward a Rhetorical Theory Accounting for Gender." *Doing Research on Women's Communication: Perspectives on Theory and Method*. Eds. Kathryn Carter and Carole Spitzack. Norwood, NJ: Ablex, 1989. 137–160.

Donaldson, Lee. "The First Woman Governor." *Woman Citizen* Nov. 1926: 7+.

Dow, Bonnie J. "Ann Willis Richards (1933–): A Voice for Political Empowerment." *Woman Public Speakers in the United States, 1925–1993: A Bio-Critical Sourcebook*. Ed. Karlyn Kohrs Campbell. Westport, CT: Greenwood, 1994. 452–464.

———, and Mari Boor Tonn. " 'Feminine Style' and Political Judgment in the Rhetoric of Ann Richards." *Quarterly Journal of Speech* 79 (1993): 286–302.

Duerst-Lahti, Georgia, and Rita Mae Kelly, eds. *Gender Power, Leadership, and Governance*. Ann Arbor: U of Michigan P, 1995.

Duffy, Barnard K., and Halford R. Ryan, eds. *American Orators before 1900: Critical Studies and Sources*. New York: Greenwood, 1987.

———. *American Orators of the Twentieth Century: Critical Studies and Sources*. New York: Greenwood, 1987.

Eagleton, Terry. *Ideology: An Introduction.* New York: Verso, 1996.

"An Ebullient Governor." *New York Times* 10 June 1984, late city ed., sec. 1: 6. Online. Lexis-Nexis, Academic Universe. 27 September 1999.

Ecroyd, Donald H. "The Agrarian Protest." *America in Controversy: History of American Public Address.* Ed. DeWitte Holland. Dubuque, IA: Wm. C. Brown, 1973. 171–184.

Ezell, Hazel F., Charles A. Odewahn, and J. Daniel Sherman. "Women Entering Management: Differences in Perceptions of Factors Influencing Integration." *Group Organizational Studies* 7 (1982): 243–253.

Field, Robert M. "Will 'Ma' Ferguson Be Impeached?" *Outlook* 9 Dec. 1925: 554–555.

Foner, Philip S., and Robert James Branham, eds. *Lift Every Voice: African American Oratory, 1787–1900.* Tuscaloosa, AL: U of Alabama P, 1998.

Foote, Jennifer. "Arizona's 'Rosie' New Boss: Mecham's Replacement Is Startling the Skeptics." *Newsweek* 22 Feb. 1988: 27.

Foss, Karen A., Sonja K. Foss, and Cindy L. Griffin. *Feminist Rhetorical Theories.* Thousand Oaks, CA: Sage, 1999.

Foss, Sonja K. "Equal Rights Amendment Controversy: Two Worlds in Conflict." *Quarterly Journal of Speech* 65 (1979): 275–288.

Frady, Marshall. "Governor and Mister Wallace." *Atlantic Monthly* Aug. 1967: 35–40.

Giddens, Anthony. *A Contemporary Critique of Historical Materialism.* 2nd ed. Stanford, CA: Stanford UP, 1995.

Goodwyn, Lawrence. *Democratic Promise: The Populist Movement in America.* New York: Oxford UP, 1976.

"Governor Barbara Roberts: Biographical Sketch." 19 Feb. 1998. <http://arcweb.sos.or.gov/governors/roberts/biography/html>.

"Gov. Hollister More than a Mere Footnote in Ohio History." *Columbus Dispatch* 8 Jan. 1999: 1A10. Online. Lexis-Nexis, Academic Universe. 3 September 1999.

"Governor Jane Dee Hull." 1 Sept. 1999. http://www.governor.state.az.us/news/indexbio4.html>.

"The Governor Lady Finds that in the East as in the West Americans Are 'Mine Own People.' " *Good Housekeeping* July 1928: 67.

"Grasso, Ella T." *Current Biography.* Ed. Charles Moritz. Vol. 36. New York: Wilson, 1975, 1976. 173–176.

"Grasso, Ella T." *Current Biography.* Ed. Charles Moritz. Vol. 43. New York: Wilson, 1982, 1983. 464.

"Grasso: Piedmont Spoken Here." *Time* 18 Nov. 1974: 10–11.

Greenblatt, Alan. "Symington Convicted of Fraud: Hull Takes Over as Governor." *Congressional Quarterly Weekly Report* 6 Sept. 1997: 2094. Online. Infotrac. Expanded Academic ASAP, Linfield College Library. 26 Sept. 1999.

Gronbeck, Bruce E. *Paradigms of Speech Communication Studies*: *Looking Back toward the Future*. Boston: Allyn, 1999.

Gruson, Lindsey. "A Familiar Role for Acting Governor." *New York Times* 7 Feb. 1988, late city final ed., sec. 1: 26.

Guttman, Robert J. "Barbara Roberts: Interview" *Europe* July-August 1993: 27–30. Online. Infotrac. Expanded Academic ASAP, Linfield College Library. 26 Sept. 1999.

Hadden, Jim. Telephone interview. 28 June 1999.

Hall, Alma. "Reflections: The Stories and Images of Women Leaders." Unpublished Diss. Vanderbilt U, 1992.

Harragan, Betty. *Games Mother Never Taught You*: *Corporate Gamesmanship for Women*. New York: Rawson, 1977.

Haywood, Charles F. "A Report on the Significance of Toyota Motor Manufacturing Kentucky, Inc. to the Kentucky Economy." Presented to the Kentucky Economic Assoc. Annual Meeting, Lexington, KY, 9 October 1998.

Hendricks, Cecilia Hennel. "When a Woman Governor Campaigns." *Scribner's Magazine* July 1928: 81–91.

Herzik, Erik B., and Brent W. Brown, eds. *Gubernatorial Leadership and State Policy*. New York: Greenwood, 1991.

Hill, Gail Kinsey. "Governor Stumps for Tax Reform." *Oregonian* [Portland] 21 Sept. 1991: D1.

———. "Political Storm Looms on Eve of Measure 5's Anniversary." *Oregonian* [Portland] 28 June 1992: A18.

———. "Roberts to Propose Two Budgets." *Oregonian* [Portland] 29 Aug. 1992: B1.

———. "State Tax Overhaul Back on Front Burner." *Oregonian* [Portland] 14 Aug. 1992: A1.

———. "Talk about Taxes." *Oregonian* [Portland] 15 Sept. 1991: A1.

Hochmuth, Marie Kathryn, ed. *A History and Criticism of American Public Address*. Vol. 3. New York: Longmans, Green, 1955.

Hoff, Joan. *Law, Gender, and Injustice*: *A Legal History of U.S. Women*. New York: New York UP, 1991.

Holland, DeWitte, ed. *America in Controversy*: *History of American Public Address*. Dubuque, IA: Wm. C. Brown, 1973.

Iker, Sam. "Changes in Dixyland." *Time* 5 Nov. 1973: 98+.

"In the First Big Test of the Negro Vote." *U.S. News & World Report* 16 May 1966: 37–39.

"Is Pa or Ma Governor of Texas?" *Literary Digest* 11 April 1925: 15.

Ivie, Robert. "Democratic Deliberation in a Rhetorical Republic." *Quarterly Journal of Speech* 84 (1998): 491–505.

Ivins, Molly. "A Texas Treasure." *Ms.* Oct. 1988: 26.

Jacobs, David. "Hollister Ready to Add to Ohio History." *The Associated Press State and Local Wire*. 30 Dec. 1998, AM cycle. Online. Lexis-Nexis, Academic Universe. 3 September 1999.

Jamieson, Kathleen Hall. *Beyond the Double Bind*: *Women and Leadership*. New York: Oxford UP, 1995.

———. *Eloquence in an Electronic Age*: *The Transformation of Political Speechmaking*. New York: Oxford UP, 1988.

———. *Packaging the Presidency: A History and Criticism of Presidential Campaign Advertising*. New York: Oxford UP, 1984.

"Jane Dee Hull." AP Candidate Bios. 1 Oct. 1998. *Associated Press Political Service*. Online. Lexis-Nexis. 20 Oct. 1998.

"Jeanne Shaheen: Biography." State of New Hampshire Office of the Governor. 10 June 1998. <http://www.state.nh.us/governor/bio.html>.

Jelinek, Estelle C. *The Tradition of Women's Autobiography from Antiquity to the Present*. Boston: Twayne, 1986.

———. Introduction. *Women's Autobiography*: *Essays in Criticism*. Ed. Estelle C. Jelinek. Bloomington: Indiana UP, 1980.

Jennings, Peter. "Introduction of Christine Todd Whitman," *ABC Breaking News*, 24 Jan. 1995.

"Joan Finney." AP Candidate Bios. *Associated Press Political Service*. Online. Lexis-Nexis. 20 Oct. 1998.

Johnson, Alicia "Women Managers: Old Stereotypes Die Hard." *Management Review* December 1987: 31–43.

Josselson, Ruthellen. *Finding Herself*: *Pathways to Identity Development in Women*. San Francisco: Jossey-Bass, 1987.

Kanter, Rosabeth Moss. *Men and Women of the Corporation*. New York: Basic Books, 1977.

Kaufman, Joanne, and Barbara Kleban Mills. "While Nebraska Governor Kay Orr Makes Policy, Husband Bill, Her 'First Gentleman,' Bakes Meat Loaf." *People Weekly* 12 Dec. 1988: 189+.

Keerdoja, Eileen, with Pamela Abramson. "Dixy Lee Ray Is Still Speaking Out." *Newsweek* 8 June 1981: 16+.

Kegan, Robert. *The Evolving Self*: *Problem and Process in Human Development*. Cambridge MA: Harvard UP, 1982.

Kennedy, Patricia Scileppi, and Gloria Hartmann O'Shields. *We Shall Be Heard*: *Women Speakers in America*, *1928–Present*. Dubuque, IA: Kendall/Hunt, 1983.

King, Janis L. "Justificatory Rhetoric for a Female Political Candidate: A Case Study of Wilma Mankiller." *Women's Studies in Communication* 13 (1990): 21–38.

Klotter, James H. Interview with Al Smith. *Comment on Kentucky*. Kentucky Educational Television, Lexington, KY. 9 Apr. 1999.

Kuhnert, Karl W., and Philip Lewis. "Transactional and Transformational Leadership: A Constructive/Developmental Analysis." *Academy of Management Review* 12 (1987): 648–657.

"Kunin, Madeleine." *Current Biography*. Ed. Charles Moritz. Vol. 48. New York: Wilson, 1987, 1988. 328–331.

Lambert, Louis. "The Executive Article." *Major Problems in Constitutional Revision*. Ed. Brooke Graves. Chicago: Public Administration Service, 1960.

Laski, Harold J. *The American Democracy: A Commentary and an Interpretation*. London: Allen and Unwin, 1949.

Leeman, Richard W., ed. *African-American Orators: A Bio-Critical Sourcebook*. Westport, CT.: Greenwood, 1996.

Lemov, Penelope. "The Decade of Red Ink." *Governing* 5 (August 1992): 22–26.

Leonard, Lee. "Seat in House Brings Hollister Full Circle." *Columbus Dispatch* 3 Feb. 1999: 5B. Online. Lexis-Nexis, Academic Universe. 3 Sept. 1999.

Lipson, Leslie. *The American Governor: From Figurehead to Leader*. Chicago: Chicago UP, 1949.

Logan, Shirley Wilson. *"We Are Coming": The Persuasive Discourse of Nineteenth-Century Black Women*. Carbondale, IL: Southern Illinois UP, 1999.

———, ed. *With Pen and Voice: A Critical Anthology of Nineteenth-Century African-American Women*. Carbondale, IL: Southern Illinois UP, 1995.

McCarthy, Nancy. "Governor Bends Ears for Tax Plan before Loss." *Oregonian* [Portland] 2 June 1992: A14.

Maccoby, Eleanor E. "Gender and Relationships: A Developmental Account." *American Psychologist* 45 (1990): 513–520.

McGee, Michael Calvin. "The 'Ideograph': A Link Between Rhetoric and Ideology." *Quarterly Journal of Speech* 66 (1980): 1–16.

———. "In Search of 'The People': A Rhetorical Alternative." *Quarterly Journal of Speech* 61 (1975): 235–249.

———. "Text, Context, and the Fragmentation of Contemporary Culture." *Western Journal of Speech Communication* 54 (1990): 274–289.

McGlen, Nancy E., and Karen O'Connor. *Women, Politics, and American Society*. 2nd ed. Upper Saddle River, NJ: Prentice, 1998.

MacKinnon, Catherine. *Toward a Feminist Theory of the State*. Cambridge, MA: Harvard UP, 1989.

"Madeleine Kunin—Governor 1985–1991." 10 Feb. 1999. <http://www.state.vt.us/governor/faq/govs/kunin.html>.

Mapes, Jeff. "Governor's Tax Plan Given Odds of Passing." *Oregonian* [Portland] 25 June 1992: A1.

———. "House Demo Chief Forecasts Ill Wind for Roberts' Tax Push." *Oregonian* [Portland] 3 Oct. 1991: B4.

———. "Roberts Finds Honeymoon Period Short." *Oregonian* [Portland] 28 Apr. 1991: B1.

———. "Roberts Not Graceful in Defeat." *Oregonian* [Portland] 12 July 1992: C3.

———. "Roberts Plots Stealthy-As-She-Goes Tax Fix." *Oregonian* [Portland] 7 June 1992: E1.

———. "Roberts Rejects Quick Fix Tax Plan to Prevent Budget Cuts." *Oregonian* [Portland] 12 Mar. 1991: B4.

Margolick, David. "Lake Lurleen Journal." *New York Times* 19 June 1991, late ed.: A16.

"Martha Layne Collins." AP Candidate Bios. *Associated Press Political Service.* Online. Lexis-Nexis. 20 Oct. 1998.

Martin, Harold H. " 'the Race of The Thousand Clowns.' " *Saturday Evening Post* 7 May 1966: 25–29.

Martin, Howard H. "President Reagan's Return to Radio." *Journalism Quarterly* 61 (1984): 817–821.

Mathews, Tom, with Paul S. Greenberg. "Washington: Lady with a Chain Saw." *Newsweek* 11 April 1977: 45.

" 'Me for Ma,' Says Texas." *Outlook* 3 Sept. 1924: 5.

"Miriam Amanda Ferguson: Soon to Take Office as the First Woman Governor of Texas." *Current Opinion* Oct. 1924: 436–438.

Misch, Georg. *A History of Autobiography in Antiquity.* Vol. 1. Trans. E. W. Dickes. Cambridge, MA: Harvard UP, 1951.

Missirian, Agnes K. *The Corporate Connection: Why Executive Women Need Mentors to Reach the Top.* Englewood Cliffs, NJ: Prentice, 1982.

Mongella, Gertrude. Foreword. *A Rising Public Voice: Women in Politics Worldwide.* Ed. Alida Brill. New York: Feminist Press-City University of New York, 1995.

Moore, Stephen. "The Real Story behind Governments' Financial Crises." *USA Today* March 1992: 10–13.

Morehouse, Sarah McCally. *The Governor as Party Leader: Campaigning and Governing.* Ann Arbor, MI: U of Michigan P, 1998.

Morrison, Ann, Randall White, and Ellen Van Velsor. *Breaking the Glass Ceiling: Can Women Reach the Top of America's Largest Corporations?* Reading, PA: Addison-Wesley, 1986.

Muhs, Angie. "Ky. Women Work Hard to Have Say in Capital." *Lexington Herald-Leader.* 14 Sept. 1998: A1+.

Mullaney, Marie. *Biographical Dictionary of the Governors of the United States, 1988–1994.* Westport, CT: Greenwood, 1994.

"Nebraska Politics." *Economist* 25 August 1990: 23. Online. Infotrac. Expanded Academic ASAP, Linfield College Library. 26 Sept. 1999.

"New Hampshire Chief Signs Gay Rights Bill." *New York Times* 8 June 1997, Sun. late ed., sec. 1: 37. Online. Lexis-Nexis, Academic Universe. 26 Sept. 1999.

O'Connor, Lillian. *Pioneer Women Orators: Rhetoric in the Ante-Bellum Reform Movement.* New York: Columbia UP, 1954.

O'Donnell, Victoria. "Dreams Can Come True for Little Girls Too: A Fantasy-Theme Analysis of Geraldine Ferraro's 1984 Acceptance Speech." *Great Speeches for Criticism and Analysis.* Ed. Lloyd E. Rohler. Greenwood, IN: Alistair, 1988. 43–54.

Oliver, Robert T. *History of Public Speaking in America*. Boston: Allyn & Bacon, 1965.

"On Political Courage, Witches, and History." *Ms.* Nov. 1987: 84.

"On the Run with Ella." *Newsweek* 4 Nov. 1974: 21.

Oravec, Christine. "The Ideological Significance of Discursive Form: A Response to Solomon and Perkins." *Communication Studies* 42 (1991): 383–391.

Osborne, David. *Laboratories of Democracy: A New Breed of Governor Creates Models for National Growth*. Boston: Harvard Business School P, 1990.

Parrish, Wayland Maxfield, and Marie Hochmuth. *American Speeches*. New York: Longmans, Green, 1954.

Parry-Giles, Shawn J., and Trevor Parry-Giles. "Gendered Politics and Presidential Image Construction: A Reassessment of the 'Feminine Style.' " *Communication Monographs* 63 (1996): 337–353.

Pedersen, Daniel. "Richards: 'I Like to Make People Laugh.' " *Newsweek* 25 July 1988: 22.

"Petticoat Politics." *Collier's* 17 April 1926: 19.

Plummer, William, and Anne Maier. "After a Mudslinging Primary, Victor Ann Richards Sets her Sights on the Lone Star Statehouse." *People Weekly* 30 April 1990: 85+.

Preece, Harold. "Ma Ferguson Wins Again." *Nation* 21 Sept. 1932: 255–256.

Pulley, Brett. "The 1997 Elections: Profile—Born with Politics in Her Veins," *New York Times* 29 Oct. 1997, late ed.: B1.

Purdum, Todd S. "Once Again in Arizona, Secretary of State Is Suddenly Thrust into the Job of Governor." *New York Times* 5 Sept. 1997, late ed.: A20.

"Quotes of the Day." *Chicago Tribune* 4 April 1995, evening update ed., sec. News: 2. Chicago Tribune Company. Online. Lexis-Nexis. 20 Oct. 1998.

Ragins, Belle R. "Barriers to Mentoring: The Female Manager's Dilemma." *Human Relations* 42.1 (1989): 1–23.

"Ray, Dixie Lee." *Current Biography*. Ed. Charles Moritz. Vol. 34. New York: Wilson, 1973, 1974. 345–348.

"Ray, Dixie Lee." *Current Biography*. Ed. Charles Moritz. Vol. 55. New York: Wilson, 1994. 660.

Rich, Bennet M. *State Constitutions: The Governor*. New York: National Municipal League, 1960.

"Richards, Ann." *Current Biography*. Ed. Charles Moritz. Vol. 52. New York: Wilson, 1991, 1992. 468–471.

Richards, Ann. "Keynote Address." Democratic National Convention, San Antonio, TX. 23 Jul. 1988.

Richards, Ann. "Remarks of Governor Ann W. Richards on the Occasion of the Inauguration." Inauguration of the Governor, State of Texas, State Legislature, Austin, TX. 15 Jan. 1991.

Richards, Ann. "State of the State Address of Governor Ann W. Richards." State of Texas, State Legislature, Austin, TX. 6 Feb. 1991.

Robbins, William. "Nebraska's Governor Bounces Back." *New York Times* 9 Feb. 1988, late city ed., A18. Online. Lexis-Nexis, Academic Universe. 27 Sept. 1999.

Roberts, Barbara. "League of Women Voters: Remarks of Governor Barbara Roberts." 18 May 1991. Ts. Governor Roberts' Papers, Box 63. Oregon State Archives, Salem, OR.

———. "Oregon Employment and Training Association Conference: Remarks of Governor Barbara Roberts." 24 Feb. 1991. Ts. Governor Roberts' Papers, Box 62. Oregon State Archives, Salem, OR.

———. "Press Release." Office of the Governor, Salem, OR. 13 Nov. 1991.

———. "State of the State Address." 23 Jan. 1992. Ts. Governor Roberts' Papers. Oregon State Archives, Salem, OR.

———. "Tom McCall Lecture Series: Remarks of Governor Barbara Roberts." 13 Feb. 1991. Ts. Governor Roberts' Papers, Box 62. Oregon State Archives, Salem, OR.

Rosenthal, Alan. *Governors and Legislatures*: *Contending Powers*. Washington, DC: Congressional Quarterly Press, 1990.

Ross, Nellie Tayloe. "The Governor Lady." Vol. 1. *Good Housekeeping* Aug. 1927: 30+.

———. "The Governor Lady." Vol. 2. *Good Housekeeping* Sept. 1927: 36+.

———. "The Governor Lady." Vol. 3. *Good Housekeeping* Oct. 1927: 72+.

Rossant, Colette. "A Visit with Vermont's Governor." *McCall's* Jan. 1988: 82–83.

Rowe, Kathleen. *The Unruly Woman: Gender and the Genres of Laughter*. Austin: U of Texas P, 1995.

Rozen, Leah, and Elinor J. Brecher. "Kentucky's New First Family Includes Another Beauty Queen—But Martha Layne Collins Is the Governor." *People Weekly* 28 Nov. 1983: 58–60.

Runnion, Marge. "Once a Refugee from Nazi Europe, Madeleine Kunin Takes Charge as Vermont's First Woman Governor." *People Weekly* 1 April 1985: 102+. Time, Inc. Online. Lexis-Nexis. 20 Oct. 1998.

Sabato, Larry. *Goodbye to Good-time Charlie: The American Governorship Transformed*. 2nd ed. Washington, DC: Congressional Quarterly Press, 1983.

Salholz, Eloise, with Karen Springen. "Are We in Kansas Anymore?" *Newsweek* 8 Oct. 1990: 34.

Salmore, Barbara G., and Stephen A. Salmore. *New Jersey Politics and Government: Suburban Politics Comes of Age*. Lincoln, NE: U of Nebraska P, 1993.

Sanford, Terry. *Storm over the States*. New York: McGraw, 1967.

Schmidt, William E. "Lincoln *Journal*: Nebraska's First Man Enjoys the Last Laughs." *New York Times* 21 Oct. 1988, late city final ed.: A14.

Schultz, Jeffrey D., and Laura van Assendelft, eds. *Encyclopedia of Women in American Politics*. Phoenix, AZ: Oryx, 1999.

"Second Time Around." *Time* 24 Sept. 1984: 31.

Shelby, Annette. "The Southern Lady Becomes an Advocate." *Oratory in the New South*. Ed. Waldo Braden. Baton Rouge, LA: Louisiana State UP, 1979. 204–236.

Sicherman, Barbara, and Carol Hurd Green, eds. *Notable American Women, The Modern Period: A Biographical Dictionary*. Vol. 4. Cambridge, MA: Belknap-Harvard UP, 1980.

Sirotu, Janet. "*McCall's* Goes to a Party: Derby Day Breakfast for 12,000!" *McCall's* April 1987: 108–111.

Skarphol Kaml, Shannon. "The People's Voice: A Comparison of Populist and Feminist Styles." Unpublished Thesis. U of Minnesota, 1996.

Smelser, Neil J. *Theory of Collective Behavior*. New York: Free Press-Glencoe, 1963.

Smith, Al. "A Baker's Dozen of Kentuckians." *Lexington Herald-Leader* 29 Mar. 1998: F1+.

Smith, Sidonie, and Julie Watson, eds. *De/colonizing the Subject: The Politics of Gender in Women's Autobiography*. Minneapolis, MN: U of Minnesota P, 1992.

Smith, Tony. *America's Mission: The United States and the Worldwide Struggle for Democracy in the Twentieth Century*. Princeton, NJ: Princeton UP, 1995.

Solomon, Martha. "Autobiographies as Rhetorical Narratives: Elizabeth Cady Stanton and Anna Howard Shaw as 'New Women.' " *Communication Studies* 42 (1991): 354–370.

———. "The 'Positive Woman's' Journey: A Mythic Analysis of the Rhetoric of STOP ERA." *Quarterly Journal of Speech* 65 (1979): 262–274.

Spitzack, Carole, and Kathryn Carter. "Women in Communication Studies: A Typology for Revision." *Quarterly Journal of Speech* 73 (1987): 401–423.

"Statewide Elective Executive Women 1999." Center for the American Woman and Politics (CAWP), National Information Bank on Women in Public Office, Eagleton Institute of Politics, Rutgers University. 1 Sept. 1999. <http://www.rci.rutgers.edu/~cwap/facts/stwide99.pdf>.

Stedman, Murray S. *State and Local Governments*. Boston: Little, Brown, 1982.

Stineman, Esther. *American Political Women*. Littleton, CO: Libraries Limited, 1980.

Stokes, Elizabeth K. Phelps. "Your Business in Washington." *Woman Citizen* 21 Mar. 1925: 7+

Stricker, Frank. "Cookbooks and Law Books: The Hidden History of Career Women in Twentieth-Century America." *A Heritage of Her Own: Toward a New Social History of American Women*. Eds. Nancy F. Cott and Elizabeth H. Pleck. New York: Simon, 1979. 476–498.

Sullivan, David B. "Challenging the Tyranny of Expectations: Women Candidates, Media, and Image-Making in Gubernatorial Campaigns." Unpublished Diss. U Massachusetts Amherst, 1995.

———. "Images of a Breakthrough Candidate: Dianne Feinstein's 1990, 1992, and 1994 Television Advertisements." *Women's Studies in Communication* 21 (1998): 6–26.

Sullivan, Patricia A. "The 1984 Vice-Presidential Debate: A Case Study of Female and Male Framing in Political Campaigns." *Communication Quarterly* 37 (1989): 329–343.

———. "Women's Discourse and Political Communication: A Case Study of Congressperson Patricia Schroeder." *Western Journal of Communication* 57 (1993): 530–545.

———, and Lynn H. Turner. *From the Margins to the Center: Contemporary Women and Political Communication.* Westport, CT: Praeger, 1996.

"Surprises from Nation's Two Woman Governors." *U.S. News & World Report* 10 Oct. 1977: 45.

Tavris, Carol. *The Mismeasure of Woman.* New York: Touchstone-Simon, 1992.

"Texas Tangled in 'Ma's' Apron-Strings." *Literary Digest* 24 Sept. 1932: 11.

Thompson, Wayne N. "Barbara Jordan's Keynote Address: The Juxtaposition of Contradictory Values." *Contemporary American Public Discourse.* Ed. Halford Ross Ryan. Prospect Heights, IL: Waveland, 1992. 279–286.

Thompson, Wayne. "Salem Dodgeball: Avoid Budget Reality." *Oregonian* [Portland] 15 Apr. 1991: B6.

Thorne, Barrie, and Zella Luria. "Sexuality and Gender in Children's Daily Worlds." *Social Problems* 33.3 (1986): 176–190.

Tolleson-Rinehart, Sue, and Jeanie R. Stanley. *Claytie and the Lady: Ann Richards, Gender, and Politics in Texas.* Austin, TX: U of Texas P, 1994.

Tonn, Mari Boor. "Militant Motherhood: Labor's Mary Harris 'Mother' Jones." *Quarterly Journal of Speech* 82 (1996): 1–21.

Toobin, Jeffrey. "How Hot Is It?" *New Republic* 7 Aug. 1989: 12–14.

Trent, Judith S., and Robert V. Friedenberg. *Political Campaign Communication: Principles and Practices,* 3rd ed. Westport, CT: Praeger, 1995.

Tronto, Joan. *Moral Boundaries: A Political Argument for an Ethic of Care.* New York: Routledge, 1993.

Twichell, Doris Yoakam. "Susan B. Anthony." *A History and Criticism of American Public Address.* Vol. 3. Ed. Marie Kathryn Hochmuth. New York: Longmans, Green, 1955.

Van Horn, Carl E. "The New Storm over the States." *The State of the States.* 2nd ed. Ed. Carl E. Van Horn. Washington, DC: Congressional Quarterly Press, 1993. 213–224.

"Vermont: Statehouse Stakes." *Newsweek* 29 Oct. 1984: 42+.

Vexler, Robert I., ed. *Chronology and Documentary Handbook of the State of Wyoming.* Dobbs Ferry, NY: Oceana, 1979.

"Wallace, Lurleen B." *Current Biography*. Ed. Charles Moritz. Vol. 28. New York: Wilson, 1967, 1968. 447–450.

Watson, Martha. *Lives of Their Own: Rhetorical Dimensions in Autobiographies of Women Activists*. Columbia, SC: U of South Carolina P, 1999.

Weatherford, Doris. *American Women's History*. New York: Prentice, 1994.

Weeks, Edward C., Margaret Halloc, James B. Lemert, and Bruce McKinlay. *Citizen Participation in Policy Formation: A Review of Governor Roberts' Conversation with Oregon*. Eugene: U of Oregon, 1992.

Welter, Barbara. *Dimity Convictions: The American Woman in the Nineteenth Century*. Athens, OH: Ohio UP, 1976.

"Whitman, Christine Todd." *Current Biography*. Ed. Judith Graham. Vol. 56. New York: Wilson, 1995. 590–594.

Whitman, Christine Todd. "Autumn Tourism." Radio Message. Office of the Governor. 4 Sept. 1998. <http://www.state.nj.us/governor/add33.html>.

Whitman, Christine Todd. "Business and Commerce." Radio Message. Office of the Governor. 25 Sept. 1998. <http://www.state.nj.us/governor/add36.html>.

Whitman, Christine Todd. "Celebrating the Best of New Jersey." Radio Message. Office of the Governor. 17 Jan. 1998. <http://www.state.nj.us/governor/news/add2.html>.

Whitman, Christine Todd. "Crime." Radio Message. Office of the Governor. 7 Feb. 1998. <http://www.state.nj.us/governor/news/add5.html>.

Whitman, Christine Todd. "Earth Day." Radio Message. Office of the Governor. 18 April 1998. <http://www.state.nj.us/governor/news/add15.html>.

Whitman, Christine Todd. "Environment." Radio Message. Office of the Governor. 14 Feb. 1998. <http://www.state.nj.us/governor/news/add6.html>.

Whitman, Christine Todd. "Family Cap and Personal Responsibility." Radio Message. Office of the Governor. 6 Nov. 1998. <http://www.state.nj.us/governor/add42.html>.

Whitman, Christine Todd. "Historic Preservation." Radio Message. Office of the Governor. 23 Oct. 1998. <http://www.state.nj.us/governor/add41.html>.

Whitman, Christine Todd. "The Inaugural Speech of Christine Todd Whitman." The War Memorial, Trenton, NJ. Tuesday, 18 Jan. 1994.

Whitman, Christine Todd. "Initiatives to Combat Crime." Radio Message. Office of the Governor. 14 Aug. 1998. <http://www.state.nj.us/governor/add30.html>.

Whitman, Christine Todd. "Iraq Military Mission." Radio Message. Office of the Governor. 18 Dec. 1998. <http://www.state.nj.us/governor/add48. html>.

Whitman, Christine Todd. "July 4th—The Promise of America." Radio Message. Office of the Governor. 4 July 1998. <http://www.state.nj.us/governor/add25.html>.

Whitman, Christine Todd. "Keeping Our Community Colleges Strong." Radio Message. Office of the Governor. 4 April 1998. <http://www.state.nj. us/governor/news/add12.html>.

Whitman, Christine Todd. "Many Faces, One Family." Radio Message. Office of the Governor. 2 Oct. 1998. <http://www.state.nj.us/governor/add38.html>.

Whitman, Christine Todd. "Mother's Day." Radio Message. Office of the Governor. 8 May 1998. <http://www.state.nj.us/governor/add18.html>.

Whitman, Christine Todd. "New Jersey KidCare." Radio Message. Office of the Governor. 28 Aug. 1998. <http://www.state.nj.us/governor/add32.html>.

Whitman, Christine Todd. "New Jersey Is Ready for Summer." Radio Message. Office of the Governor. 15 May 1998. <http://www.state.nj.us/governor/add19.html>.

Whitman, Christine Todd. "One Million Acres!" Radio Message. Office of the Governor. 30 Oct. 1998. <http://www.state.nj.us/governor/add40.html>.

Whitman, Christine Todd. "Open Space." Radio Message. Office of the Governor. 9 Oct. 1998. <http://www.state.nj.us/governor/add37.html>.

Whitman, Christine Todd. "Open Space." Radio Message. Office of the Governor. 17 July 1998. <http://www.state.nj.us/governor/add27.html>.

Whitman, Christine Todd. "Open Space." Radio Message. Office of the Governor. 24 Jan. 1998. <http://www.state.nj.us/governor/news/add3.html>.

Whitman, Christine Todd. "Our Open Space Legacy." Radio Message. Office of the Governor. 26 June 1998. <http://www.state.nj.us/governor/radio/add24.html>.

Whitman, Christine Todd. "Personal Responsibility." Radio Message. Office of the Governor. 4 Dec. 1998. <http://www.state.nj.us/governor/add46.html>.

Whitman, Christine Todd. "Personal Responsibility." Radio Message. Office of the Governor. 10 Jan. 1998. <http://www.state.nj.us/governor/news/add1.html>.

Whitman, Christine Todd. "Remarks of Governor Christine Todd Whitman, Second Inaugural Address." Newark, NJ. 20 Jan. 1998. <http://www. state.nj.us/governor/speeches/inaug 98. html>

Whitman, Christine Todd. "Remembering Our Fallen Heroes." Radio Message. Office of the Governor. 23 May 1998. <http://www.state.nj.us/governor/add20.html>.

Whitman, Christine Todd. "School Safety." Radio Message. Office of the Governor. 11 Sept. 1998. <http://www.state.nj.us/governor/add34.html>.

Whitman, Christine Todd. "Services for Seniors." Radio Message. Office of the Governor. 7 Aug. 1998. <http://www.state.nj.us/governor/add29.html>.

Whitman, Christine Todd. "Serving New Jersey's Veterans." Radio Message. Office of the Governor. 13 Nov. 1998. <http://www.state.nj.us/governor/add43.html>.

Whitman, Christine Todd. "State Plan." Radio Message. Office of the Governor. 28 Feb. 1998. <http://www.state.nj.us/governor/news/add8.html>.

Whitman, Christine Todd. "Summer Safety." Radio Message. Office of the Governor. 21 Aug. 1998. <http://www.state.nj.us/governor/add31.html>.

Whitman, Christine Todd. "Thanksgiving Message." Radio Message. Office of the Governor. 28 Nov. 1998. <http://www.state.nj.us/governor/add45.html>.

Whitman, Christine Todd. "Tourism." Radio Message. Office of the Governor. 1 May 1998. <http://www.state.nj.us/governor/add17.html>.

Whitman, Christine Todd. "TTF and Open Space Consensus." Radio Message. Office of the Governor. 24 July 1998. <http://www.state.nj.us/governor/add28.html>.

Whitman, Wilson. "Can a Wife Be Governor?" *Collier*'s 5 Sept. 1925: 5–6.

Williams, Dennis A., with Michael Reese. "Can Dixy Rise Again?" *Newsweek* 14 July 1980: 28.

Williams, J. Oliver. "Changing Perspectives on the American Governor." *The American Governor in Behaviorial Perspective*. Eds. J. Oliver Williams and Thad L. Beyle. New York: Harper and Row, 1972.

Witherspoon, Patricia D. *Communicating Leadership: An Organizational Perspective*. Boston, MA: Allyn, 1997.

———. "We the People: Barbara Jordan's Statement before the House Judiciary Committee on the Impeachment of Richard M. Nixon." *Great Speeches for Criticism and Analysis*. Ed. Lloyd E. Rohler. Greenwood, IN: Alistair, 1988. 183–194.

"Woman's 'Bigger Dent in Politics.' " *Literary Digest* Nov. 22, 1924: 17.

"Women Who Won on November 4th." *Woman Citizen* 15 Nov. 1924: 9.

Wren, J. Thomas. *Leaders' Companion: Insights on Leadership through the Ages*. New York: Free Press, 1995.

"Wyoming's Woman Candidate." *Literary Digest* 1 Nov. 1924: 13.

Yoakam, Doris. "An Historical Study of the Public Speaking Activity of Women in America from 1828–1860." Unpublished Diss. U of Southern California, 1935.

———. "Woman's Introduction to the American Platform." *A History and Criticism of American Public Address*. Ed. W. Norwood Brigance. Vol. 1. New York: McGraw-Hill, 1943. New York: Russell & Russell, 1960.

Zaeske, Susan. "The 'Promiscuous Audience' Controversy and the Emergence of the Early Woman's Rights Movement." *Quarterly Journal of Speech* 81 (1995): 191–207.

Zorn, Theodore E. "Construct System Development, Transformational Leadership and Leadership Messages." *The Southern Communication Journal* 56 (1991): 178–193.

Index

About the Contributors

ALMA HALL serves as chair and Assistant Professor in the Department of Communication Arts at Georgetown College. Holding an MSW from the University of Louisville and graduate communication courses from Western Kentucky University, she returned to Vanderbilt University for her doctorate after careers in social work and business. Her dissertation, "Reflections: The Images and Stories of Women Leaders," extended her interest in leadership studies. She continues to provide communication team building and leadership consulting for nonprofit and business development. She recently published an article in *The Advocate* entitled "Defender Professionalism and Excellence," based on leadership consulting with an agency of the Kentucky state government. Dr. Hall maintains affiliation with the National Communication Association, the National Society for Experiential Education, and several business organizations.

SHANNON SKARPHOL KAML is a Ph.D. candidate in the Department of Speech Communication at the University of Minnesota. Her research interests include public address, social movement, and visual communication. A portion of her dissertation is published in the 1999 Proceedings of the NCA/AFA Conference on Argumentation. She is the recipient of the University of Minnesota's Arle and Billy Haeberle Research Award and Top Four Paper awards from both the National Communication Association's Visual Communication Division and the Central States Communication Association's Communication Theory Division.

BRENDA DeVORE MARSHALL is an Associate Professor and Chair of the Department of Theatre and Communication Arts at Linfield College in McMinnville, Oregon. She received her Ph.D. in Speech Communication and Theatre from Southern Illinois University–Carbondale in 1988. Her research interests include women's rhetoric, gendered communication, feminist theory and intercultural communication. She currently serves as Linfield's Title IX Officer.

MOLLY A. MAYHEAD is a Professor of Speech Communication at Western Oregon University in Monmouth. She received her Ph.D. from Penn State University in 1988. Her research interests include Supreme Court rhetoric, First Amendment issues, and women's rhetoric. She is extremely active in the local teacher's union in which she serves as grievance officer. She resides on a four-acre farm with her husband, Ed Dover, two cats, and her dog.

JENNIFER BUREK PIERCE earned a Ph.D. in rhetorical studies and an MLS from Indiana University in 1999. She is the reference librarian at the National Center for Education in Maternal and Child Health, Georgetown University. She also teaches both composition and communication classes, most recently at Indiana University and St. Mary-of-the-Woods College. Her research focuses on women's public political roles in the 1920s, particularly as reflected by women's magazines of the time. She currently lives in Virginia with her husband and two cats.

KRISTINA HORN SHEELER is a Visiting Lecturer and Doctoral Candidate in Speech Communication at Indiana University. Her dissertation, titled "Women's Public Discourse and the Gendering of Leadership Culture: Ann Richards and Christine Todd Whitman Negotiate the Governorship," is the basis for her essays. At Indiana University she teaches courses in interpersonal communication, business and professional communication, and persuasion.